# NEGRO MINSTRELS

## a complete guide

### Jack Haverly

*LITERATURE HOUSE / GREGG PRESS*
Upper Saddle River, N. J.

Republished in 1969 by
*LITERATURE HOUSE*
an imprint of The Gregg Press
121 Pleasant Avenue
Upper Saddle River, N. J.  07458

Standard Book Number—8398-0771-6
Library of Congress Card—74-91099

# THE AMERICAN HUMORISTS

Art Buchwald, Bob Hope, Red Skelton, S. J. Perelman, and their like may serve as reminders that the "cheerful irreverence" which W. D. Howells, two generations ago, noted as a dominant characteristic of the American people has not been smothered in the passage of time. In 1960 a prominent Russian literary journal called our comic books "an infectious disease." Both in Russia and at home, Mark Twain is still the best-loved American writer; and Mickey Mouse continues to be adored in areas as remote as the hinterland of Taiwan. But there was a time when the mirthmakers of the United States were a more important element in the gross national product of entertainment than they are today. In 1888, the British critic Grant Allen gravely informed the readers of the *Fortnightly*: "Embryo Mark Twains grow in Illinois on every bush, and the raw material of *Innocents Abroad* resounds nightly, like the voice of the derringer, through every saloon in Iowa and Montana." And a half-century earlier the English reviewers of our books of humor had confidently asserted them to be "the one distinctly original product of the American mind"—"an indigenous home growth." Scholars are today in agreement that humor was one of the first vital forces in making American literature an original entity rather than a colonial adjunct of European culture.

The American Humorists Series represents an effort to display both the intrinsic qualities of the national heritage of native prose humor and the course of its development. The books are facsimile reproductions of original editions hard to come by—some of them expensive collector's items. The series includes examples of the early infiltration of the autochthonous into the stream of jocosity and satire inherited from Europe but concentrates on representative products of the outstanding practitioners. Of these the earliest in point of time are the exemplars of the Yankee "Down East" school, which began to flourish in the 1830's— and, later, provided the cartoonist Thomas Nast with the idea for Uncle Sam, the national personality in striped pants. The series follows with the chief humorists who first used the Old Southwest as setting. They were the founders of the so-called frontier humor.

The remarkable burgeoning of the genre during the Civil War period is well illustrated in the books by David R. Locke, "Bill Arp," and others who accompanied Mark Twain on the way to fame in the jesters' bandwagon. There is a volume devoted to Abraham Lincoln as jokesmith and spinner of tall tales. The wits and satirists of the Gilded Age, the Gay Nineties, and the first years of the present century round out the sequence. Included also are several works which mark the rise of Negro humor, the sort that made the minstrel show the first original contribution of the United States to the world's show business.

The value of the series to library collections in the field of American literature is obvious. And since the subjects treated in these books, often with surprising realism, are intimately involved with the political and social scene, and the Civil War, and above all possess sectional characteristics, the series is also of immense value to the historian. Moreover, quite a few of the volumes carry illustrations by the ablest cartoonists of their day, a matter of interest to the student of the graphic arts. And, finally, it should not be overlooked that the specimens of Negro humor offer more tangible evidence of the fixed stereotyping of the Afro-American mentality than do the slave narratives or the abolitionist and sociological treatises.

The American Humorists Series shows clearly that a hundred years ago the jesters had pretty well settled upon the topics that their countrymen were going to laugh at in the future—from the Washington merry-go-round to the pranks of local hillbillies. And as for the tactics of provoking the laugh, these old masters long since have demonstrated the art of titillating the risibilities. There is at times mirth of the highbrow variety in their pages: neat repartee, literary parody, Attic salt, and devastating irony. High seriousness of purpose often underlies their fun, for many of them wrote with the conviction that a column of humor was more effective than a page of editorials in bringing about reform or combating entrenched prejudices. All of the time-honored devices of the lowbrow comedians also abound: not only the sober-faced exaggeration of the tall tale, outrageous punning, and grotesque spelling, but a boisterous Homeric joy in the rough-and-tumble. There may be more beneath the surface, however, for as one of their number, J. K. Bangs, once remarked, these old humorists developed "the exuberance of feeling and a resentment of restraint that have helped to make us the free and independent people that we are." The native humor is indubitably American, for it is infused with the customs, associations, convictions, and tastes of the American people.

PROFESSOR CLARENCE GOHDES
*Duke University*
*Durham, North Carolina*

January, 1969

The minstrel show, in which white male performers with cork-blackened faces impersonated Negroes, appeared in America early in the nineteenth century. About the turn of the century, Negroes shared comic roles with "stage" Irishmen and "stage" Yankees, but no attempt had been made to present "Negro life"—even in caricature—to the public. Minstrels first appeared in interludes between plays in the legitimate theater. These lively little sketches became increasingly popular and eventually provided an entire evening's entertainment.

An enterprising actor named Thomas Rice is credited with staging the first full-fledged minstrel show. Rice had been fairly successful as a blackface comedian. One day in 1828 in Cincinnati, he heard a black man or a street urchin—the accounts differ—singing this ditty:

> Step first upon yo' heel
> An' den upon yo' toe,
> An' ebry time you turns around
> You jump Jim Crow.
> Next fall upon yo' knees
> Then jump up and bow low
> An' ebry time you turn around
> You jump Jim Crow.

He jotted down the words, worked up a song-and-dance routine, and in the true American spirit of big-scale promotion, made a fortune in productions bearing savory titles such as *Jumbo Jim, The Virginia Mammy,* and *Bone Squash Diavolo.* The term "Jim Crow," which today means any sort of discrimination against black people, came out of Rice's shows. Rice himself played the role of "Jim Crow": a shuffling, obsequious Kentucky-cornfield Negro in Solon Robinson's play *The Rifle.* Rice played this part with great success in Louisville, Cincinnati, Philadelphia, New York, and London. In London the chimney sweeps and apprentices were quick to imitate Jim's limping dance.

"Christy's Minstrels," the most renowned of the early shows, was established in Buffalo in 1842. Edwin P. Christy used many of Stephen Foster's beautiful tunes, and his minstrels played to packed houses in England and America for a decade.

Henceforth, the minstrel show generally followed the pattern set by Christy. In the first part, a single row of "Negroes" (Haverly's "Burnt-Cork Brotherhood") was seated on chairs. The humor consisted of exchanges between the "interlocutor," a "straight man," and Tambo and Bones, the "end men." There were also mock lectures and sermons of the sort written by William Levison. The humor—for it certainly could not be called wit—was lowbrow and leaned heavily on puns, the most childish form of verbal amusement. It was not obscene, if we can judge from surviving collections.

The second act, the "olio," was a variety entertainment made up of banjo players, clog dancers, perhaps a watermelon man. According to an English reviewer, Jack Haverly's "American and European Mastodon Minstrels" sang comic Irish songs—pretty far from de ole plantation!

The show concluded with an "after-piece," another variety entertainment. It frequently played up the combination of simplicity and low cunning attributed to Negroes by the all-white audiences. (Negroes were prohibited from acting in or attending these shows.) The "after-piece" also parodied popular plays, operas, and important persons.

Innumerable minstrel troupes toured the United States and Europe from 1850 until the First War. Although the genre died out in the 'twenties, it continued to influence radio shows ("Amos 'n' Andy," Rochester in "The Jack Benny Show") and performers such as Al Jolson. Contemporary Negro writers and a few movie producers are trying to efface the image of the black man which minstrel shows impressed upon the minds of white Americans for almost a century: the "darky shuffle," the atrocious dialect, wide lips, gold teeth, etc.

The great historian of the drama, Arthur Hobson Quinn, thought that "The main strength of negro minstrelry lay in its musical and picturesque extravagance, and its significance as drama is slight. Had it been the result of negro initiative it would have been more important, but in its inception it was burlesque rather than sincere imitation. . . ." And *The American Negro Reference Book* comments: "On the positive side, however, the white blackface minstrels introduced to the American public the entertainment values inherent in Negro material—before Negroes themselves could appear on Jim Crow stages."

*Upper Saddle River, N. J.*                                    F. C. S.
*May, 1969*

# Negro Minstrels

A COMPLETE GUIDE TO NEGRO MINSTRELSY, CONTAINING RECITATIONS, JOKES, CROSS-FIRES, CONUNDRUMS, RIDDLES, STUMP SPEECHES, RAGTIME AND SENTIMENTAL SONGS, ETC., INCLUDING HINTS ON ORGANIZING AND SUCCESSFULLY PRESENTING A PERFORMANCE.

BY

## JACK HAVERLY.

—

Chicago

FREDERICK J. DRAKE & COMPANY

Publishers

# Negro Minstrels

Nothing gives the amateur such rare opportunities for displaying talent as a negro minstrel performance. Anyone with but little study and practice can successfully entertain an audience and keep them in roars of laughter for hours by the aid of this volume.

Negro minstrels can be easily organized and with but a small expense. Nothing can give an audience a more highly pleasing entertainment than a minstrel show. It is always appreciated to such an extent that everyone is more than satisfied for the amount paid for the price of admission.

## ORGANIZING.

Be careful in the selection of your middle and end men.

Your middle man must be possessed with a great deal of dignity and also speak in a clear distinct voice so that the entire audience will hear his repeating or reply of every line spoken by end men. He must also refrain from laughter, if possible. In the selection of end men who take part as *Bones* and *Tambo*, choose one man who is sarcastic in nature, another who is droll and slow in speech, another who is fat and jolly, another who is well qualified for recitations, etc. All must be naturally bright and witty, so that they can catch everything going on both on the stage and in the audience. Singing of

comic songs and using good negro dialect are also es
sential with all end men.

1 will add that the success of the show generally de-
pends on the middle man. It is his duty to arrange the
sayings of end men, songs or ballads of the singers, etc.
He must always announce to the audience each one's part.
Viz: Mr. Wilson will now sing that beautiful ballad, "A
Rose of a Hundred Leaves," or Mr. Sweatman, How are
you feeling this evening, etc., etc. When Bones or Tambo
desire to speak or tell a conundrum they will address the
middle man: "Mr. Johnson (or any name) can you tell
me the difference, etc." By following these rules your
performance is a positive success.

Always remember at the rise of the curtain everyone
in the company should be standing and at the close of
the opening chorus the middle man will instruct you with
the remark, *"Gentlemen, be seated."*

## ARRANGEMENT OF THE STAGE.

Always cover the chairs to be occupied by the end
men and middle man with some cloth material so they
will be distinguished from the balance of the company.
*See frontispiece.* If you have plenty of stage room it
will add greatly to the appearance of the opening part
by having your orchestra on a raised platform of about
18 inches. This, however,, is not essential.

## HOW TO MAKE UP.

Take a quantity of corks, place them in a tin pail or
dish, saturating them with alcohol, then light. Let them
burn to a crisp, when burned out, mash them to a pow-
der, mix with water to a thick paste place the mixture in
small tin boxes and it is ready for use. In applying it to

your face it is better first to rub the face and hands with cocoa butter, which can be purchased from any druggist at a small cost, as when removing the black it can be rubbed off easily with a dry cloth. It is not necessary to use carmine for the lips to make them appear large. All that is required when applying the black is to keep it about one-half an inch away from the mouth, or more if a larger mouth is wanted. This only applies to end men. The balance of the company should black close to the lips so as to appear dignified and neat in appearance.

## REGARDING WIGS.

It is better for the amateur to buy wigs ready made. Any dealer in theatrical goods or publishers of plays can furnish them at a small cost. End men should always get comic wigs for their parts. The balance of the company should wear nothing more than a regular dignified wig. By following these suggestions, you will find that your performance will be successful.

## COSTUMES.

End men appear to best advantage when they dress in a neat but flashy costume, consisting of knee trousers made of black cloth or satin, a swallow tail coat of red or some bright color with vest to match; white or colored shirt with large wing collars, patent leather, low-cut shoes, and black stockings. The balance of the company should wear only black evening dress, white shirts and white neckties, thereby assuming a very dignified appearance.

## ADVERTISING.

Nothing succeeds so well as judicious advertising. First prepare your programme of just such acts as you intend presenting for the opening night, using as much display as possible and also, if procurable from your local printer, get humorous darkey cuts to insert upon it—thereby making it attractive or something that will not be immediately thrown away. Then proceed to bill your town, carefully covering every house, store, shop, etc., including surrounding territory of at least five miles. Start these circulars out not less than twenty days before the performance. Also have your local newspaper write you up daily regarding your rehearsals, etc. You will find only standing room upon your opening night if these instructions are carried out.

## PROPERTIES.

Every well regulated minstrel show should appoint some one in the company to act as property man. It will be his specific duty to care for all articles used on the stage, such as chairs, umbrellas, brooms, tables, or any accessories needed by the artists in their or his act. These properties should always be kept in a handy place, so that they can be procured in a moment's notice.

## REHEARSALS.

Rehearsals should be given as often as four times a week, so as to commit to memory everything in conversations, songs, gags, jokes, etc., that passes between the middle man and the end men. All of the songs and chorus should be practiced with the orchestra. so that perfect time is rendered with the music. Never hurry things in a minstrel performance, as you are sure to lose the desired effect upon your audience.

## FIRST PART.

Open your performance with a song by the company. Then proceed with some gags from the end-men, immediately following with a sentimental ballad from one of the singers. When finished, have one of the end-men say a few pleasing remarks regarding it. Follow this with a coon song (rag time) and dance; follow with more jokes, songs, etc., and close the first part with a rag time song and chorus.

## PROGRAMME.

### HAVERLY'S MASTODON MINSTRELS.

Bones—Mr. Wallace.     Tambo—Mr. Sweatman.
Bones—Mr. Wilson.      Tambo—Mr. Tate.
Middle-Man—Mr. Cleveland.

---

### GRAND OPENING POTPOURRI.

Opening Chorus ......................Entire Company
Song by Tenor...........................Mr. Wilson
Comic Song, Gags, etc...................Mr. Wallace
Baritone Song and Chorus...............Mr. Stafford
Funny Story..........................Mr. Sweatman
Song—Alto ..............................Mr. James
Comic Song, Gags, etc.................Mr. Cleveland
Recitation—Comic ........................Mr. Tate
Finale—*Ain't Dat a Shame*............Four End-Men
Chorus by Company.

---

### PART II.

Stump Speech .........................Mr. Wallace
Song and Dance..................Cleveland and Tate
Banjo Solo, Songs and Sayings..........Mr. Sweatman
Intermission.
Orchestra . ............................Sousa March
Sketch ............................Wallace and Tate
Concluding with that side-splitting farce,

### BLACK MAIL,

An original negro comicality.

Professor Coon...........................Mr. Wallace
Marcillus ................................Mr. Tate
Gus Blue ..............................Mr. Sweatman

---

Doors Open at 7:30.     Performance Commences 8:15,
Admission 25c.

## A WOMAN AND AN UMBRELLA.

"Why is a woman like an umbrella?"

"Because she's made of ribs and attached to a stick."

"Wrong. Guess again."

"Because she always has to be shut up when——"

"Naw! You fatigue me."

"Because she stands in the hall and——"

"Naw! It's nothing about standing in the hall."

"A woman is like an umbrella because nobody ever gets the right one."

"Ring off! That isn't the answer, either."

"It's a better one than you've got."

"Don't you rockon I know whether it is or not? Whose conundrum is this, yours or mine?"

"Well, she's like an umbrella because—it isn't because she fades with age, is it?"

"You ought to be ashamed of yourself."

"I am. Is it because you have to put up when it's cloudy and threatening—no, that can't be it. Because she's a good thing to have in the house."

"You're not within four counties of it."

"Because you can't find any pocket in either."

"No choice. Vote again."

"I won't! A woman isn't like an umbrella. There is not the slightest resemblance."

"I knew you couldn't guess it. It's because she's accustomed to reign."

## A NEW JOB.

Mr. Cleveland, I got a new job since I saw you.

Mid.—What doing?

End.—Holding cows for a cross-eyed butcher.

Mid.—How did you like it?

End.—Oh, I didn't like it at all.  You see, the first cow I held the butcher drew off to hit her (you know how a cross-eyed man looks); I said, "Say, are you going to hit where you're looking?"   (I thought he was looking at me.)   He said, "Yes."   I said, "I guess you'll have to get some one else to hold your cow."

## NEVER READ BEFORE MEALS.

Mr. (name some one in the audience) went into a restaurant the other day and when the waiter gave him a bill of fare, said:  "Thank you, I never read before meals."

## LOST TWO CHILDREN.

Mid.—Here is something for poetry composition I reserved for you both:  Mr. Brown, a policeman, lost his two children—twins; now, compose something on that.

2d End.—We"l do it together.

1st End.—"Policeman Brown, of our town,
    Was blessed with a pair of twins;
One had a cough which took it off,
    From this abode of sins."

2d End.—"And number one had scarcely gone,
    (Into his coffin slid),
When number two went up the flue,
    To join the other kid."

## GOOD SINGING.

End.—Mr. Cleveland, I love to hear good singing; especially the old songs. For instance: "The Old Folks at Home."

Mid.—Yes, and I love to be with the old folks at home.

End.—Well, I don't blame you; it beats working for a living. And another good old song: "Way Down Upon a Shanghai's Liver."

Mid.—You mean, "Way Down Upon the Suwanee River."

End.—Is that it? You know I used to be quite a singer myself, and I sang to a very large audience.

Mid.—Did you meet with success?

End.—No, I met with a tomato. There was a very kind-hearted gentleman in the audience wanted to present me with a basket of tomatoes; he couldn't reach the stage, so he thought he would present them to me at a distance, one at a time. The first one struck me right here; he aimed for my heart and I never saw a tomato splatter so in my life. I looked up to see from whence it came and I got another right here (*points to nose*).

Mid.—Struck you in the face?

End.—No; on the end of my face—on my proboscis—right on my face handle, and it came near destroying my smelling apparatus. It came with such force, I felt it on the back of my neck. It was one of the very worst tomatoes I ever saw. I don't see how it ever held together until it reached me.

Mid.—Perhaps it was a case tomato.

End.—It was one of the worst cases of tomato I ever saw.

Mid.—Oh! well, let it go by.

End.—I only wish it had gone by.

## A GIRL FROM 'FRISCO.

Mid.—My girl came clean from San Francisco to see me.

End.—It's about time she came on clean, for she is the dirtiest-looking girl I ever saw.

---

## WHAT'S IN A NAME?

End.—Mr. Cleveland, does yo' know Mary?

Mid.—Mary?

End.—She's a berry lively gal.

Mid.—Mary who?

End.—Mary-land.

End.—Mose, does yo' know Sal?

End.—Sal?

End.—She's a nice gal, an' you' ought ter know her.

End.—Sal who?

End.—Sal—vation.

End.—Mr. Cleveland, yo' fell down stairs yes'day.

Mid.—I did, from the top to the bottom.

End.—Yo' must hev been hurt, as I heerd yo' call fo' Helen.

Mid.—I did not call for Helen.

End.—Yes yo' did.

Mid.—I did not.

End.—Yes yo' did—I heeru yo'.

Mid.—Call for Helen? Helen who?

End.—Helen Blazes.

Everyone.—Oh, Mr. Cleveland!

## HE DIDN'T FEEL GOOD.

Well, Smith, how do you feel to-day?

Why, Doctor, I don't feel any better.

Did you get the leeches?

Yes; but I only took three of them raw; I had to get my wife to fry the rest.

---

## SWEET KISSER.

End.—That girl of yours is a sweet kisser.

Mid.—How do you know?

End.—Oh, I had it right from her own lips.

---

## HOW TO MAKE SHOES.

End.—I understand that you are a shoemaker. Now how would you go to work to make a first-class pair of shoes?

Mid.—Why, I'd make the soles of the best oak leather, the uppers of the best French kid and I'd line them with lamb's wool. There, sir, is a pair of shoes that can't be beat.

End.—Those would be good State street shoes. But I'll tell you how to make the best pair of shoes that you ever saw. I'd make the uppers of drunkard's throats. They'd be warranted never to take water. I'd line them with young lover's hearts. They'd always be warm and comfortable. The soles——

Mid.—What would you make the soles of?

End.—I'd make the soles of old maid's tongues, because they'd be everlasting and never wear out.

## COMES IN AHEAD.

Mid.—I saw you out driving the other day. That was a very spirited animal you had.

End.—The fastest in the world.

Mid.—What's his name?

End.—Brains.

Mid.—Brains? I never heard of him.

End.—He always comes in ahead (a head).

---

## STLYE.

End.—I bought a hat for my wife and I had to run home all the way.

Mid.—What for?

End.—I was afraid the style would change before I got home.

---

## KNEED 'EM.

End.—Mr. Cleveland, why are men like dough?

Mid.—Because they are apt to rise.

End.—No, sah.

Mid.—Then because some are light, and some are heavy.

End.—No *sah*.

Mid.—Then why *are* men like dough?

End.—Because de women (k) need 'em.

---

## A STUDY IN ASTRONOMY.

Mid.—Jake, did you ever study astronomy?

End.—ɪes sah. I'se studied my gal, who is a regular Venus.

Mid.—Then perhaps you know why the moon is called "she?"

End.—Bekase she has a sun, who comes rolling home in de mornin'.

Mid.—You cannot blame him, when his mother gets full. An' stays out all night.

End.—Dat's whar her money goes. She often has only a quarter.

Mid.—Why are a girl's thoughts like the moon?

End.—Kase dar's a man in it.

## THE DEVIL.

End.—Oh, Mr. Cleveland.

Mid.—Well, Sam, what agitates you?

End.—If de debble should lose his tail whar'd he giter nudder?

Mid.—Where would he get another? Why, in a cheap saloon, of course.

End.—An' why so sah?

Mid.—Because in cheap saloons they *retail bad spirits.*

End.—Speakin' ob de ole boy, I has one fo' yo', Mr. Cleveland.

Mid.—Name it, James.

End.—Why am de debble like a pawnbroker?

Mid.—Because you go to both when you are hard up.

End.—An' den dey's got him fast.

End.—How you make dat out, yo' brack rascal?

End.—Co'se de debble an' de pawnbroker bofe claim de unredeemed.

## WANTS.

End.—Mr. Cleveland, kin yo' tell de difference 'tween a man's wants an' a woman's wants?

Mid.—I'm afraid not.  Can you?

End.—Sartin.  A man wants all he kin git.

Mid.—And a woman?

End.—A woman wants all she can't get.

---

## A STRONG WIND.

Mid.—Did you hear about the accident that occurred to my wife the other day?

End.—No, what was it?

Mid.—We were walking down the main thoroughfare and a gust of wind came and blew a lady's hat off and hit my wife's eye; and do you know it cost me twenty dollars for doctor's fees.

End.—A similar accident happened to my wife.  She was going by a millinery store and a hat struck her eye and it cost me fifty dollars.  (I'd rather have her go by (buy) the store than go by the hat.)  I'll never forget the last time I was in court.

Mid.—Why so?

End.—I went in the court-house just as the judge was passing sentence on two Chinamen and an Irishman. The judge said to the Chinaman, "Stand up; what is your name?"  The Chinaman said, "Ha Sin."  The judge said, "Ha Sin, ten days."  And he said to the next Chinaman, "What is your name?"  The Chinaman said, "Ha Fun."  The judge said, "Ha Fun, ten days."  He said to the Irishman, "Stand up; what is your name?'' The Irishman said, ''Ha, H——; give me ten days.''

Mid.—Well, that was equalizing things pretty well.

End.—Well, you know everything will equalize itself eventually.

Mid.—How so?

End.—The rich man will have ice in the summer and the poor man will have it in the winter.

---

## "THE MISSING UMBRELLA."

End.—I saw you in church last Sunday. I was there, I contributed towards the new window they're going to put in the colored church. I believe it's necessary these warm nights.

Mid.—I dare say you have reformed in a great many things. You do not steal any more chickens?

End.—No, indeed. I've joined church.

Mid.—Nor any turkeys?

End.—No, sir. I tell you I've reformed.

Mid.—Nor any geese?

End.—No, sir; no geese.

Mid.—I am glad to hear that.

End. (to man next to him)—If he had said ducks he'd a had me. But say, I lost my umbrella that day, but I didn't make a fuss over it. I just got up and said, ''Brethren and sistern, I've lost my umbrella. I know who took it. If my umbrella isn't returned to me by next Sunday I'll get up here and mention the name of the man that stole my umbrella.

Mid.—What was the result?

End.—Next morning my yard was full of umbrellas.

## TAIL A WAGGIN'.

End.—We were going so fast when out driving the other day that we smashed into another team and it took a wheel off the dog's tail.

Mid.—Nonsense; who ever heard of a wheel on a dog's tail. Wagons have wheels.

End.—Well, this dog's tail was a "waggin'."

---

## EVERYBODY SATISFIED.

End.—Did you know the old man was dead?

Mid.—Is that so? What complaint?

End.—No complaint; everybody was satisfied.

---

## AROUND YOUR NECK.

End.—That's a nice collar you've got on. I'll bet I know where you got it.

Mid.—Where?

End.—Around your neck.

---

## HE SWALLOWED AN EGG.

End.—I'm in an awful fix. You know I'm fond of eggs, and if I can't buy any I'll steal them.

Mid.—I know you are an all around poultry thief.

End.—Well, I was over in the market and I had just picked up an egg and before I could hide it in my pocket along came the owner of the egg stand. So I quick put the egg in my mouth. I thought it was safe there. The man came along and he says, "Hello, Charley," and he slapped me on the back. That made me swallow the egg. It's in me yet. Oh! I'm in an awful fix.

Mid.—Why?

End.—If I sit still the egg will hatch. If I move around the egg will break and cut me all to pieces with the egg shell. Oh! and if it hatches there will be a great big shanghai rooster inside of me scratching for corn.

---

### AN OPERATION.

Mid.—I saw a wonderful operation to-day; the surgeon took a lung out of a man.

End.—That's nothing; I know a wife that left her husband, and she took the heart out of him.

---

### BUSINESS.

End.—Mr. Cleveland, I hear dat you's gone inter de milk business.

Mid.—That's quite true, and I am very successful.

End.—I jedge so. I saw yo' buyin' a lot er chalk dis mo'nin'.

Mid.—That's to *chalk* down your account, for you never pay.

End.—Well who would pay fo' ole skim milk?

Mid.—I do not skim my milk.

End.—Yes yo' do. Yo' skims it on top an' den yo' turns it ober an' skims it on de bottom.

Mid.—I hear that you have opened a jewelry store.

End.—Am dat so? When, when was it?

Mid.—Last night, with a crowbar.

## A VARIETY OF FISH.

End.—I say, Mr. Cleveland, did yo' ebber fink dat fish am like folkses?

Mid.—I don't know that I ever did.

End.—Well sah, dey am, fo' a fac'.

Mid.—Can you give us a few illustrations?

End.—Wiv de mos' excrutiatin' pleasure.

Mid.—Well, then, what is a rich man?

End.—He's a *gold* fish.

Mid.—Very good.   And what would you call a fat man?

End.—He's a *whale*.

Mid.—What would you call a great actor?

End.—He's a *star* fish.

Mid.—What is a dude?

End.—A dude is a *weak* fish.

Mid.—What is a lawyer?

End.—A lawyer am a *shark*.

Mid.—What is my little boy?

End.—He's a *sun* fish.

Mid.—What is a mean, selfish, ugly man?

End.—A *dog* fish, ebbery time.

Mid.—And what is Sam?

End.—A big *cat* fish, more mouf dan brains.

Mid.—And what would you call me?

End.—You?   You's a rum-*sucker*.

---

## TWO AND ONE SMELT.

End.—I has a queernundrum fo' yo', Mr. Cleveland.

Mid.—Go ahead, James.

End.—A man bought two fish an' when he got home

found he had three fish. Does yo' ketch on?

Mid.—No. I fail to see the point. How was it?

End.—He had two fish—an' one smelt.

---

## SUPERSTITIOUS.

End.—Mr. Cleveland, are you surper—are you sura-tion—are you supa——?

Mid.—You mean superstitious.

End.—That's it; I never could say superstitious. Do you believe in horseshoes over doors, etc.?

Mid.—Yes, I do. I have a shorseshoe over my door, and I have had good luck ever since.

End.—So do I. I nailed a horseshoe over my door and the next day someone stole my wife.

Mid.—I suppose you took it down after that?

End.—No, sir; nailed another one up.

Mid.—What for?

End.—I want them to come after my mother-in-law.

---

## FLY PAPER.

Mr. Cleveland, I saw Mr. — (name some one in the audience) going by a drug store the other day and saw some fly paper in the window full of flies. He went in and asked: "How much will you take for that currant pie?"

---

We started home on a street car one day and he was carrying a big basket of provisions home. I told him to set it down on the platform. He said: "No, sir; the horses have enough to do to carry me."

## BRICKS ENOUGH.

End.—Casey is a smart Irishman. He was building a
house and he didn't have money enough to buy any more
bricks. Right across the way they were building another
house and there was a big pile of bricks and a gang
of Irishmen working. Casey tried his best to steal some
of them, but it was no use.

Mid.—"Thou art so near and yet so far."

End.—Yes. Casey thought of a plan. Next day he
got up on his fence and yelled "Hurrah for the A.
P. A."

Mid.—What was the result?

End.—He got enough bricks to build two houses.

---

## EDITOR OF A PAPER.

End.—Say! I fell out of bed last night.

Mid.—You slept too near where you got in.

End.—No; I slept too near where I fell out.

Mid.—You expect the unexpected in circumstances of
that peculiarity.

End.—What's the matter with you; you've changed
your boarding house again, haven't you?

Mid.—Is it possible that my hyphenated sentences are
entirely too complex for the intellect contained in that
diminutive cocoanut?

End.—Hold on, you allegorical hypothesis; don't give
me any of your chin music. I know something about
language myself, for I started a paper once. It was
called "Blood"—but it had very poor circulation. It
was a tri-weekly—it came out one week and tried to
come out the next. Where's your brother, the editor?

Mid.—A horse ran away with him and he's been laid up for two weeks.

End.—Same thing happened to my brother. He ran away with a horse and he's been laid up for two years.

Mid.—What became of your newspaper?

End.—Busted up. All the old maids in town would go around and tell the news before I could print it.

## LOOKED LIKE A DUDE.

Mid.—You don't look like you did last winter; when I saw you then, you looked like a dude.

End.—Times are different; I'm married now.

Mid.—What has married life to do with it?

End.—Why, I'm sub-dued now.

## GETS DUNNED.

Mid.—I wonder where Jones is this evening; it's time he were here. Ah, here he is. [Enter Jones, excited.] We were just now wondering where you were.

End.—That so? Been out on a snap dis arternoon—didn't get froo till dark.

Mid.—Why, you had a long bill, then.

End.—How did you know we had him along wid us?

Mid.—Had who? I didn't mention anybody's name.

End.—Yes, you did; you said we had Long Bill.

Mid.—I wasn't aware that there was any performer by that name.

End.—Oh, yes; he's a long-haired Indian scalper; he does a war dance. But, Jim, talk about your Long Bills, we had longer bills den him round us afo' we left town; took every *red* I had.

Mid.—Why, you astonish me. I was not aware that you was in the habit of running up bills.

End.—No, I nebber run up bills; bills run me down; but dere was a kind of sumpin' about dese bills dat made us skwurm.

Mid.—What kind of men were these that would compel a man to pay a bill that he did not owe?

End.—They warn't men.

Mid.—Warn't men? What were they, women?

End.—What? women? Go 'way; what do you take me for? Of course, dey wasn't women.

Mid.—What were they, then?

End.—Mosquitoes, and dey performed a great miracle wid me.

Mid.—Indeed; what was it?

End.—Why, you see, dem mosquitoes, aldo' dey didn't eat my flesh, when 'em got froo wid me dere was nothing but *Jones* left.

---

## WHO IS THE MOTHER?

Mid.—Say, Bones, I want to ask you a question. Now, suppose I go down to market, and buy a dozen fresh eggs; I bring them home, and I get a hen to hatch them. Now, who is the mother of these chickens? The one that laid them; or the one that hatched them?

End.—Why, the one that laid them, of course.

Mid.—No, sir! The one that hatched them is the mother. If she had not hatched them, they would never have existed, never have been born.

End.—I say that the hen that hatched them was simply hired out as a wet nurse, and the one that laid them was the mother. Say, for instance, I go down to the market and I get a dozen duck eggs, and I get a hen to hatch them. Now, is she the mother of those ducks? Did you ever see a hen lay ducks?

---

## "OH GIRLS."

End.—My brother has a matrimonial agency! Come around if you want to get married. He'll pick out a good wife for you.

Mid.—Thank you. I'm afraid he could not select a wife to suit me.

End.—He's got all kinds. He can tell you just what they are and how good they are by their names.

Mid.—By their names only?

End.—Yes, their characters and dispositions. For instance:

A good girl to have, *Sal Vation*. A disagreeable girl, *Annie Mosity* A fighting girl, *Hittie Maginn*. A sweet girl, *Carrie Mel*. A very pleasant girl, *Jennie Rosity*.

Mid.—How about a stylish girl?

End.—Why, *Ella Gant*. A musical girl, *Sarah Nade*. A lively girl, *Annie Mation*. A clear case of girl, *E. Lucy Date*. A seedy girl, *Cora Ander*. A clinging girl, *Jessie Mine*. A serene girl, *Mollie Fy*.

Mid.—A warlike girl?

End.—*Millie Tary!*

Mid.—The best girl of all?

End —Your own girl, of course.

Mid.—I've got you; a great big fat girl?

End.—(Laughs.) *Ella Phant*.

## THE GAMBLER.

Mid.—Do you know John Euchre?

End.—Do you mean John Euchre, the gambler?

Mid.—Yes; the poor fellow died yesterday, and I want you to compose something appropriate. Take your time about it.

End.—I can give it to you right now. I don't have to study it over. Let's see—John Euchre, gambler. Here you are: A gambler's life is easily explained. First, he tries to *go it alone* He's *a trump* if he's on the square. He *cuts* a *good deal* with a *pack* of friends and often *calls* on everybody to *raise* money, principally from his *ante,* or *sees* his uncle. He's often at the *clubs,* wears *diamonds* and plays for *hearts.* Finally he *lays down his hand* and allows a *spade* to turn him down in the *flush* of life. If he has been *straight* he *wins* the *game,* though it may be his last *shuffle.* He's got to *cash in his chips,* for the *bluff* is over and he's *euchred* at last.

---

## ARRESTED FOR CHEATING.

I was in court the other day and I saw two men who were arrested for cheating a man out of one hundred dollars, and the Judge said: "Stand up and state your case."

"Well, I will tell you, your Honor, my friend and I, we got playing a game of cards and my friend bet this man that he could bring out two Jacks together, and the cards were shuffled up and by mere accident the two Jacks came our together."

The Judge said: "What is your name?"

"Jack Brown."

"And what is your name?"

"Jack Smith."

The Judge said: "Jack Brown, I'll give you six months, and you, Jack Smith, I'll give you one year; and I'll bet one hundred dollars that you two Jacks don't come out together."

## GUESS AGAIN.

Mid.—Mr. James, have you any cash to-night?

End.—Let me see—Yes I hab a dollar and some cents

Mid.—Ah! some *sense?* Well, that will keep you from spending the dollar for whiskey.

End.—Well, Mr. Cleveland, I had some sense de oder night.

Mid.—How so, Mr. James?

End.—Why, I took my gal to a garden concert one night las week, an as she looked berry dry, I asked her if she wouldn't hab sumting to drink.

Mid.—Well?

End.—She replied dat she was as dry as an empty jug! I said what'll you hab? She replied, Well—I guess—I guess—I'll hab champagne!

Mid.—What did you say to that?

End.—I tole her *to guess again.*

## THE EARTH'S AXIS.

End —Mr. Cleveland, a fellow was trying to stuff me dat when it am night here it am day in China.

Mid.—Well, James, that is true.

End.—What makes it true?

Mid.—It is caused by the earth revolving on its axis, and—

End.—What am an axis?

Mid.—Why an imaginary line on which—

End.—What am an imaginary line?

Mid.—A line passing through the center of the earth.

End.—But it don't, does it?

Mid.—Of course not; it only—

End.—How does the earth revolve, then?

Mid.—Why, on its axis.

End.—But you said it didn't hab any axis

Mid.—No, I didn't; I said the axis was an *imaginary* line—

End.—What's imaginary?

Mid.—Now you keep still, I'm talking. The earth's axis.

End.—What axis?

Mid.—James, your head is too thick to understand what is meant by the earth's rotation, but—

End.—What's rotation?

Mid.—Why, it's—it's—the—er—here, you just rotate out of this and don't bother your wooden head about things that don't concern you. Now for the next thing on the program.

----

## FIGURES SOMETIMES LIE.

End.—Can you tell me how many feet dare am in one yard?

Mid.—Yes, a linear yard contains three, a square yard nine, and a cubic yard twenty-seven feet.

End.—Can't dare be mo dan twenty-seben feet in any yard?

Mid.—No!

End.—Dat's whar you're off.  Our barn-yard hab got ten cows in it, and each cow hab got four feet, dat makes *forty feet*.

---

## GET ON TO THE DOG.

Mid.—When are you going to get married, Tambo?

End.—Not until sealskin sacks go out of fashion.

Mid.—By the way, Tambo——

End.—No, buy the beer; that will be better.

Mid.—I was going to ask you what has become of your little dog.

End —Oh, you mean Towser!

Mid.—Yes; you know I liked that dog, and I have every reason to believe that he liked me.

End.—I took notice there was a kindred feeling between you.  I had him out some time ago exercising, and I took him through the park.  We came across a bench; on this bench sat two little fleas.  One flea said to the other: "Get on to the dog."  He has been full of fleas ever since.

---

Are those apples fit for a hog to eat?

Try one and see.

---

## A JAIL-BIRD.

End.—Dere's a ting dat hab been puzzling me, Mr. Cleveland.

Mid.—Well, what is it, Mr Wallace?

End.—Why do dey call a thief a jail-bird?

Mid.—Because, I suppose, he has been so often in

prison that he may be considered to have made his nest there.

End.—Dat am no *sell,* am it?

Mid.—Certainly not! It is a plain answer.

End.—It won't do for me, though.

Mid.—Why not?

End.—Because dey call a thief a jail-bird when he's been *a robin.*

---

## A FISHY JOKE.

End.—He! He!! He!!! Mr. Cleveland, can you tell why fishermen possess extraordinary powers?

Mid.—I am afraid that your nautical knowledge is beyond me.

End.—Because dey *cure dead fish.* He! He!!

Mid.—Why this continued levity?

End.—Ah, it am a funny thing, you know, dis fifth letter of de alphabet.

Mid.—Fifth letter of the alphabet? Yes, with the aspirate prefixed.

End.—You may be *as pirati*cal as you please, but you can't *aspire* to my meaning. Now, why am de fifth letter of de alphabet—he! he!! hee!!!—like—he! he!!—like death?

Mid.—I acknowledge that you have me there.

End.—Because it am the *end of life.* He-he-he-hee-e-e-hee!!!

Mid.—Now, if you can stop giggling long enough I would like your attention to this question: What is the greatest conundrum?

End.—I hab to give dat up.

Mid.—Well then, the greatest conundrum is *Life,* because we all have to give it up.

## MR. CLEVELAND ON LAWYERS.

End.—Mr. Cleveland, would you like to be a lawyer?

Mid.—No, I do not admire the profession.

End.—Wouldn't you like to be like a lawyer?

Mid.—No, I am glad I am not even like a lawyer, because first they *lie* on one side, and then they *lie* on the other, and are wide awake all the time.

End.—Yes, but you don't know what lawyers do when dey am dead.

Mid.—I suppose they do nothing then.

End.—Oh, don't dey dough?

Mid.—What can they do when they're dead?

End.—Well, when dey're dead, you see, dey *lie* still.

## OPINION OF MATRIMONY.

Mid.—What is your opinion of matrimony, Mr. Sweatman?

End.—My opinion of matrimony? Well, I tink it am someting like a cold shoulder of mutton. I'd much rather do widout it if I could help it.

Mid.—Then your opinion is not a high one?

End.—Nor am de shoulder ub mutton a *high* one, I hope.

Mid.—And when did you come to your conclusion about matrimony?

End.—Soon after I got married.

Mid.—After the honeymoon, I suppose.

End.—Yes. Mr. Cleveland, can tell me de difference between a honeycomb and a honeymoon?

Mid.—I should not think there could be a great deal

of difference, as they are both supposed to be so very sweet.

End.—Oh, are dey?

Mid.—So it is said.

End.—I know better. De difference between a honey-comb and a honeymoon am dis, de honeycomb am made of a lot of little *cells,* but de honeymoon am one enormous *sell* altogeder.

---

## GET OFF.

I got on the train to go to Boston; the conductor was a friend of mine; we used to go to school together. When he came around for tickets I told him I left my purse on the piano and had no money with me. He said: "Oh! that's all right; get off."

---

End.—I say, Mr. Cleveland, you know Bill Jones, don't you?

Mid.—Yes, of course I do.

End.—Bill, my brother and myself we went into a restaurant where they had beer on draught, and we all sat right in the draught. After we got through draught-ing, we had a dispute as to who would pay for it, and we came to the conclusion to blindfold the landlord and the first one of us three he caught would pay for the drinks.

Mid.—Who did he catch?

End.—None of us yet. I've been living out in the country since I saw you last, but I didn't like it; the only comfort I had was a quiet room; I slept in a regis-ter bed.

Mid.—What kind of a bed was that?

End.—A slat fell out every hour, only four slats in the bed. If I went to bed at twelve, I found myself on the floor at four. Then they had a bad habit of waking people up at half-past four every morning.

Mid.—What did they wake you that early for?

End.—They used the bed sheets for table cloths. But the surroundings of the hotel kept me awake all night; so many bull frogs. I could hear them all night (*imitates frogs*). And the cow frogs made more noise than the bull frogs.

Mid.—Cow frogs? I never heard of such a thing.

End.—The idea! never heard of cow frogs. So much ignorance and so many free schools. Why a cow frog is a bull frog's sister. Everything annoyed me so, I thought I would leave the hotel, so I hitched up a carriage that was in the room and drove off.

Mid.—Hitched up a carriage that was in the room and drove off? Did you sleep in a barn?

End.—I didn't sleep with you, did I?

Mid.—No; but explain yourself?

End.—Well, you see, the bed was a little buggy, and I had the nightmare, so I hitched the mare to the buggy and drove off.

---

## THE JEALLUSEST OB HER SECT.

Mid.—As we are all here we will call upon Mr. Wilson to tell the public "what he knows about courting."

End.—H'ya! h'ya! Yes, I'se been dere, for certain, but I can't say dat I was always de lucky feller dat I ought to be. In fac' de last 'casion I tried it on was bilked.

Mid.—You floored her with a *billet*, I suppose, and

was driven away from her father's house by your *maiden speech.*

End.—My *maiden's "peach?"* O, *she* didn't peach; I did it all myself. You know a feller sometimes gits tired of his own wife, and mine am de most jeallusest ob her sect. She's always pullin' de wool ober my eyes in one way or anudder. De way it happen was dis:—Jus' roun' de corner from our house libs about the pootiest gal dat eber you did seen. She was tall as a big sunflower, and as full of cemetery as—as de Wenus ob Medicine.

Mid.—Be more careful! The Venus of Medici, sir.

End.—Well, it's all de same—dey was both on 'em wirgins—*wergin' onto forty,* dat is to say. Well, de gal she 'cipricate my tender passion, an' I *tender* her my heart an' han', and *tend her* to de freeayter and de smash balls, till de poor gal was as crazy as a bedbug, an' I wasn't much better. I writ her a letter, and de pore gal she *po* [*u*] *red* ober it, it was so affectin', till it was wet wid her tears. Well, de ting went on swimmin'ly for a while, but one day I come home suddenly and foun' de old woman *swimmin' in tears.*

Mid.—You might say *drowned* in tears, if you'd thought of it.

End.—And I was *bathed* in perspiration. She'd been intersectin' one o' my billy duxes—

Mid.—A *pretty duck* you must have been to permit it. But ventilate, sir—ventilate.

End.—Well, I never *went-till-late* to see my Phillis, and dat's de way I s'pose I fell into de hands ob de *Phillistines.* Dat night I slip into de gal's back parlor, as usual. It was as dark as her face in dere, and she'd ax'd me to whisper, so de folks couldn't hear us. Dere we sot huggin' and kissin' and makin' vows ob eternal debility to each oder, an' I presentin' her wid candies an' sweetmeats, and dat kind o' tings. Says she, kind o' singin'—"It must go werry hard on your poor wife." "O," says I, "don't you mind her; she's an old scarecrow, anyway." Wid dat she gib *went* to a yell like an Injen on de war path and *went* for me at de same time. Jus' den de do' *busted* open and she *busted* into tears, and I *busted* der snoot of a feller dat come in at dat moment wid de light—

Mid.—Came in with *delight*, sir? What do you mean?

End.—No, no—wid de candle—and den she scream till she *busted* her corsets wid rage, and I *busted* out ob de room and went on a *bust*, and would you b'lieve it, it wasn't my gal at all, but *my wife!* She'd persuaded my Phillis' fader to send her away and cum in her place. I was seventy-five cents out on her, too, and dat was all I got for it. Tinks I, nebber mind, I fixes you for dat, bime-by, presently. So what does I do but when she says she'd be dere nex' night agin I takes along wid me a big bag ob somethin', and dere I find her su' enough, sittin' alone in de dark. "Gub us a kiss," said I, and wid dat I made a rush for her and emptied a whole bag ob flour ober her, till she looked as if she'd been takin' a bath o' whitewash. De woman yelled like a stuck pig, and raise de house, an' dey all *rushed* in wid *rushlights* in der hands, and that blest if it wasn't *my gal herself*, arter all! Nebber felt so cheap in all my life—nebber, nebber! Hasn't spoke to me since.

## DE MUDDER OF INWENTION.

"Eph, I'm getting werry economical, now."

"You are?"

"Yes."

"Why, Pete, that is something new for you."

"Yes, Eph; but den you see dat necessity's de mudder of inwention; and I've proved dat it's so."

"In what manner?"

"Why, I've inwented a plan to make a leg ob mutton last a whole week."

"A whole week?"

"Yes, sir."

"How do you do it?"

"I'll tell you——

> On Sunday, being a feast day boasted,
> I like a leg ob mutton roasted;
> On Monday den my taste to tickle,
> I eat it cold wid some pickle;
> On Tuesday I broil it wid due care,
> And mashed pertatoes do prepare;
> On Wednesday, bake a season pie,
> If not enough, some slices fry;
> On Thursday, I hab some hash made,
> Around de dish some toast is laid;
> On Friday, I pronounce a fast,
> Den Saturday, when de cash gets narrow—"

"What, then?"

"I crack de bone, and eat de marrow."

---

## SIX DOLLARS OUT OF THREE.

Mid.—I can make six dollars out of three. (*Takes three silver dollars out of pocket.*)  I never hung around

a postoffice two hours trying to slip a letter in, **either.**
You see! There are six dollars!

End.—You're foolish; there's only three dollars!

Mid.--Well, I can make six out of them.

End.—Let's see you do it.

Mid. (*counts the dollars*).—One! Two! Three! (*then
back again*) One! Two! Three! (*which makes the first
one count three, he then says*): "Three and two are five
and one (*indicating the first one*) are six.

End. (*kind of puzzled*).—Well! Well! That's so, but
I can do more than that with them. I can divide them
equally.

Mid.—That is impossible, unless you get them changed.

End.—No, sir; I'll divide them equally without getting them changed or splitting them.

Mid.—Well, if you can do that, I will give you half.

End. (*takes the three dollars from the Interlocutor,
counts them as he did, to make six, and says*):—Now,
then, take three from six and it leaves three. I'll keep
these three and you can have the other three.

---

End.—I saw you with a lady the other **day. Who is**
she?

Mid.—That is my young lady.

End.—Do you like her?

Mid.—Why, certainly I do.

End.—Well, you can have her.

Mid.—Do you not think she is good looking?

End.—Well, I must say, if I was seeking for a good
looking girl I'd skip her.

Mid.—Why, she is only sixteen years old, a young
girl.

End.—This is her second time on earth. Young! young!! Why, the wrinkles in her face are large enough for flies to hide in. Her face looks like quarter past six. You darn't take her and that face out Sunday?

Mid.—Why not?

End.—If you did, she'd break the Sabbath.

Mid.—I want you to understand that that face grew on her.

End.—Well! I'm glad it didn't grow on me.

Mid.—She is a stylish girl. Did you take notice of her carriage?

End.—She was riding in a wheel-barrow when I saw her.

Mid.—No! No! I mean her walk.

End.—Oh, her walk. Well! if there is one thing I do admire more than another, it is a lady with a good walk. It saves car fare.

Mid.—Did you take notice how she glides along?

End.—She's got to glide. She can't lift them; her feet are that big. (*Measures with two hands about half a yard.*)

Mid.—Do not go too far.

End.—She can't go far with them feet.

---

## SOMETHING ABOUT UMBRELLAS.

End.—I lost a beautiful silk umbrella yesterday

Mid.—Did you leave it anywhere?

End.—No, the man that owned it came along and took it out of my hand. I hear that they are going to make *square* umbrellas.

Mid.—Umbrellas in square shape. What is that for?

End.—So you won't leave them *round*. Did you ever

notice how people carry umbrellas? Of course, you've heard of the handkerchief flirtation. Well, umbrellas tell the story of the people who carry them.

Mid.—Give me a simile.

End.—For instance, if you see a man with an umbrella, and he's very careful of it, keeps his eye on it all the time; that's a sign he's just acquired it and is afraid of losing it himself. If you see a couple going along the street, and he carries the umbrella in such a way that she is thoroughly protected and *he* gets all the rain down his neck and over his new clothes; that's a sign that they are courting. They're in love!

Mid.—Yes?

End.—And if he carries the umbrella so she gets soaking wet, and the umbrella covers him; why, they're *married.*

Mid.—Suppose it isn't his wife?

End.—Then I'll bet ten dollars *it's his mother-in-law.*

---

## MOMENTOUS QUESTION.

End.—What makes a little dog wag his tail?

Mid.—Because he is glad to see his master.

End.—No; it's because de dog is stronger dan de tail; if de tail was de strongest it would wag de dog, wouldn't it, say?

Mid.—Yes; but suppose de little dog had no tail to wag?

End.—Well, den he would have to fall back on his own jurisdiction, and hire some oder little dog to wag his for him.

## CHARGE FOR "EATING BY WEIGHT."

End.—Funny hotel I stopped at near Kokomo. They weighed you before you went into the dining room and they weighed you when you came out.

Mid.—They charged by weight?

End.—Yes. They had scales outside of the dining room and they weighed you. First time I went in they weighed me and I couldn't eat anything, for I felt sick, but they put me on the scales and weighed me. They charged me three dollars.

Mid.—That was robbery.

End.—Yes, but I was bound to get even. Next day I loaded my pockets full of brickbats. I says to the landlord, "Weigh me, weigh me." He put me on the scales and made a note of it, and I went into the dining room. Oh, how I did eat. I ate from soup to walnuts. After I had eaten I took all the bricks out of my pocket and slipped them under the table. Then I walked out to the landlord and said, "Weigh me; weigh me."

Mid.—What was the result?

End.—The landlord owed me seven dollars and a half.

---

## HIS OWN GRANDFATHER.

I tell you, Mr. Cleveland, I have been in a lot of trouble lately.

Mid.—Tell us all about it.

End.—I don't know who I am.

Mid.—Do not know who you are?

End.—Na, I don't. (*Commences to cry.*)

Mid.—I am sorry. Tell us all about it?

End.—I will, there is quite a story connected with it.

Years ago I married a widow who had a grown up daughter. My father visited us often, fell in love with my step-daughter and married her. Thus he became my son-in-law, and my stepdaughter become my mother, because she was my father's wife. Soon after this my wife gave birth to a son, which, of course, was my father's brother-in-law and my uncle, for he was the brother of my step-mother. My father's wife also became the mother of a son. He was, of course, my brother, and also my grand-child, for he was the son of my daughter. Accordingly, my wife was my grandmother, because she was my mother's mother. I was my wife's husband and grandchild at one and the same time, and, as the husband of a person's grandmother is his grandfather, I became my own grandfather.

---

### A KISSING BEE.

End.—I was down to a kissing-bee some time ago.

Mid.—Kissing bee; why, I never heard of such a thing. Explain yourself.

End.—Well, I'll tell you. A denomination of people get together at this bee, and they charge you so much for kissing, and all the money goes to some charitable institution.

Mid.—Well, what do they charge to kiss a little girl about ten years old?

End.—Ten cents.

Mid.—What do they charge to kiss a young lady of about eighteen?

End.—Fifty cents.

Mid.—What do they charge to kiss another fellow's girl?

End.—One dollar.

Mid.—What do they charge to kiss a married lady?

End.—And her husband there?

Mid.—Yes.

End—Two dollars.

Mid.—Well, what do they charge to kiss an old maid?

End.—Two for a quarter.

------

## "HAS NOT CAUGHT ME YET."

End.—I went with a friend to the (name the one in your town) hotel and we had a grand banquet. Beef all over mud, cold slush, pickled eel's feet, humming birds' tongues. Oh, all the delicacies in season and out of season. You can tell how much we eat; the bill was twenty-eight dollars, and there was only three of us. Of course we each wanted to settle the bill. Jake wanted to pay for it. Si wanted to pay for it, and I wanted to pay for it. We couldn't agree, so I proposed a plan. That was to call in the waiter, blindfold him, and whoever he caught was to pay the bill.

Mid.—That was a just way to settle the argument.

End.—Yes; so we called in the waiter, blindfolded him, and turned him loose.

Mid.—Who did he catch?

End.—I don't know. He hasn't caught me yet.

------

## IGNORANCE.

1st End.—Sam, yo's jest de ignorantest culled pusson I ebber seed.

2nd End.—I knows jest as much as yo' do, any day.

1st End.—Get out! Yo' haven't as many brains as a hog.

Mid.—Here, this won't do. We can have no quarreling here.

1st End.—I don't car'. He *haint* got es many.

Mid.—How do you make that out?

1st End.—Easy enough. He has only his head full, while a hog has a hogshead full.

---

## WHO CAME FIRST.

End.—Where did a hen's egg come from?

Mid.—From the hen, of course.

End.—Where did the hen come from?

Mid.—From the egg.

End.—Who came here first?

---

## MISSED THE BOAT.

End.—Say, I saw you last summer going home feeling coo happy for any use. You were taking up all the sidewalk and part of the road, shouting at the top of your voice: "Hip! Hip! Hurrah! I'm a whale!" and singing: "I won't go home till morning." A policeman grabbed you and you didn't get home for thirty days.

Mid.—I think I was going to that great excursion when I saw you.

End.—Excursion? Oh, I wish you hadn't mentioned that here. Every time I think of that excursion it brings tears to my eyes. (*Commence to cry.*)

Mid.—Well, Bones, I am very sorry I spoke about it. What is the trouble? What happened?

End.—Didn't you hear about it?

Mid.—Na; what was it?

End. (*cries ad libitum*)—Oh! Oh! Well, I'll tell you about it. Just as I got to the wharf, everyone was on board anticipating a great time. Band was a playing, everyone was waving their handkerchiefs, and the boat hadn't been gone no more than twenty minutes when the boiler burst, and you never saw so much hash in your life.

Mid.—Were none of the passengers saved?

End.—Not one soul was saved. There was a few old shoes floated ashore and that's all. (*Cries loudly.*)

Mid.—Well, perhaps your brother or a sister was on board?

End.—No! oh, No. (*Cries louder.*) I didn't know a soul on board.

Mid. (*indignantly*)—Well, what are you crying for?

End.—Because my mother-in-law missed the boat.

---

## WHY A SHIP IS LIKE A WOMAN.

End.—Did you know that I was one of the very first volunteers that went off to Manilla.

Mid.—Army or Navy?

End.—Navy. I didn't want any of that army beef.

Mid.—Were you on a gun-boat or a man-of-war?

End.—I was on a woman of war?

Mid.—You mean man-of-war.

End.—I mean *woman of war*. Now, suppose you saw a vessel approaching, decorated with flags, how would you express admiration?

Mid.—I should say *she* was a magnificent craft.

End.—There you are. How can *she* be a *he?* Therefore it must be a woman, for she has *bows* and a *waist*. It takes a *man to manage her*. A ship is like a woman, for it *brings news from abroad*. She always makes up to a *pier*. She runs after a *smack,* she's ridiculous when in company of small *buoys*. She's sometimes in company with a *man-of-war* And last of all, a woman is like a ship because the *rigging* costs more than the *hull*.

---

## FISHING.

End.—Why is a young lady like going fishing?

Mid.—Why is a young lady like going fishing? I am sure I don't know. I don't believe she is.

End.—Yes she is. A young lady is exactly like going fishing. Her eyes are the fish line, her smiles the bait, her kisses the hook, and matrimony is the frying pan in which the poor sucker is cooked, and his mother-in-law stands by to see that he's "well done."

---

## MARRIAGE.

A man that is thirty-five marries a girl of five years of age; he is just seven times as old as she. He lives with her five years, which makes her ten and himself forty; now he is four times as old as she. He lives with her ten years longer, which makes her thirty and him sixty; now he is twice as old as she. Figure that up and tell me how long he has to live with her before they are of the same age.

## MISSED THE FUNERAL.

End.—I lost five dollars the other day, Sam!

Mid.—How was that?

End.—Well, you know, old man Wallace, he died; when he was dying, he made out his will. He divided his money equally with his family and then he kept ten dollars over to give to the pall-bearers to buy liquor with. They asked him if they would spend it before or after the funeral. He said, "Spend it going out there. For I'll not be with you coming back." He also willed five dollars apiece to each pall-bearer, providing they followed the hearse to the cemetery without lifting their eyes from the ground, and for every time one of them looked up to fine him one dollar. Myself and Jimmie Skipper were two of the pall-bearers, and we started with our hands over our eyes, following the hearse, determined to earn our five dollars. We walked about a mile. When I commenced to smell the vilest kind of a smell. I said to Jimmie, "What in the world is that smell? I can't stand it." He said: "For goodness sake don't look up or he'll fine you a dollar." Well, I walked along a while, but I couldn't stand that smell any longer. So I said, "You look up, and if he fines you a dollar I'll go halves with you." So he looked up. He said to me, "You can look up, too, it's all right." I looked up, and what do you think, Sam?

Mid.—What?

End.—We'd followed a swill cart for the last half a mile.

## YES OR NO.

Mr. Cleveland; when I come to look at you, you rascal, I honestly think you're the finest looking man I ever saw.

Mid.—Thank you, Tambo; I am sorry I cannot return the compliment.

End.—You could, if you told as big a lie as I did.

Mid.—I suppose you think you are smart, don't you?

End.—No, sir; I ain't half as smait as the man that's twice as smart as I am. But, leaving all jokes aside, I'd like to make a wager with you, that you can't answer "yes" to three questions I ask you.

Mid.—Certainly, I can. That is easy enough.

End.—Well, I'll bet you a bottle of wine that you can't.

Mid.—It is a go. Gentlemen, you understand; it is a bottle of wine, that I cannot say "yes," to three questions he asks me.

End.—That's right. Now, here goes: Were you ever in jail?

Mid.— (hesitates).—Yes!

End.—You were? Well, I didn't know I was in that kind of company.

Mid.—Never mind; that is one for me, anyhow.

End.—Well, suppose you should meet a poor, little, emaciated, half-starved boy in the street, and some good, kind person had just given him a piece of bread. With the fierce eagerness of hunger, he is about to devour this bread. Could you have the heart to snatch that bread from him, and see him die at your feet of starvation?

Mid.— (hesitates; at last very reluctantly says.)— Yes.

End.—Oh, you double-dyed villian! You old, hard-shell human vampire! Where do you expect to die when you go to! Oh, you flint-hearted monster!

Mid.—Here! here! Never mind that. That's two for me. You have only got one more chance.

End.—Well, say, if I lose this bet, will you pay for the wine?

Mid. (*quickly*)—No.

End (*all laugh*)—Ha! ha! You've lost.

---

## A SMOKY CHIMNEY.

Mid.—Mr. Wilson, I have got a chimney that smokes very badly, do you know what will remedy the difficulty?

End.—You can bet, I do.

Mid.—Why, did you ever see one cured?

End.—Seen it! I think I hab. I once had de very worst chimbley I eber see, and I cured it a little too much.

Mid.—How was that, Bones?

End.—Why, you see, Mr. Cleveland, I built a little house out yonder, at Wolf Hollow, ten or twelbe years ago. Jim Bush, de good-for-nuffin' fellow dat built de chimbleys, kept blind drunk three-quarters ob de time, and crazy drunk de udder. I tole him I thought he'd have somethin' wrong; but he stuck to it, an' finished de house. Well, we mov'd in, an' built a fire de next morning, to boil de tea-kettle. All de smoke came in de room, an' went out ob de windows; an' not a bit went out ob de flues. We tried it for two or free days, an' it got worse an' worse. By-and-by, it came on to rain,

an' de rain began to come down de chimbley. It put
de fire out in a minute, an' directly it came down by de
pailful. We had to get de baby off de ground as soon as
we could, or it would hab been drowned. In fifteen
minutes de water stood knee-deep on de floo'. I soon
saw what was de matter. De drunken cuss put de chimbley wrong end up, an' it drawed downward. It gathered
all de rain within a hundred yards, an' poured it down
by bucketfuls.

Mid.—That *was* unfortunate; surely, you never cured
that chimney?

End.—Well, I guess I did!

Mid.—How?

End.—Turned it de udder side up, an' den you ough'ter
seen it draw. Dat was de way I cured it too much.

Mid.—Drew too much? How was that?

End.—Well, you may judge for yourself. Soon after
1 got de chimbley down, t'other end up, I missed won
ob de chairs out ob de room, an' directly I seen anudder
ob dem shooting for de fireplace. Nex' de table went,
den de back log. Den I grabbed de ole woman under
one arm, an' de baby under de udder, an' started; but
as I got to de doo' I seen de cat goin across de floo'
backward, holdin' on wid her claws to de carpet, yellin'
awfully. It wasn't no use, Mr. Cleveland, I jus' see her
goin' ober de top ob de chimbley, an' dat was de las' ob
her.

Mid.—Well, what did you do then? Of course you
could not live in such a house?

End.—Well, you jes' bet I did! I put a blister on de
jam' ob de fireplace—one ob dem porous ones, you know,
an' dat drawed de udder way, so we had no more
trouble.

## LETTERS AT THE POST OFFICE.

End.—I thought I saw you out at the baseball game. They've got a new pitcher. His name is *Dice*; but they found Dice hard to *rattle*.

Mid.—What is your brother doing at present?

End.—Getting rich by collecting hush money from every family in town.

Mid.—Hush money!

End.—Yes; he manufactures *soothing syrup*. All of our family are smart. If they wanted to find out anything they'd come to us. If anything was lost they'd come to our house to find it. We knew everything and everybody. Did you know that everybody resembles a letter in the post office? Everybody, men, women and children—are letters, especially the ladies.

Mid.—What kind of a letter is a married lady?

End.—She's a letter that has *reached its destination*.

Mid.—What kind of a letter is a young lady?

End.—She's a letter that *hasn't been sent yet*.

Mid.—What kind of letters are babies?

End.—They are merely *litle postal cards*.

Mid.—What kind of a letter is a fat lady?

End.—She's *overweight* and *collect postage*.

Mid.—What kind of a letter is an undertaker?

End.—He has charge of the *dead letters* only.

Mid.—What kind of letters are old maids?

End.—Letters that have been overlooked in the *General Delivery*.

---

## VEGETABLES.

Mid.—I know a man in California that raised a pumpkin so large that his two children use a half each for a cradle.

End.—That's nothing; we have in this town, as many as three policemen sleeping on one beat.

---

End.—My wife stole a cradle to-day.
Mid.—What for?
End.—Oh, just for a kid.

---

End.—Say, Joe, I'm in a new business now!
Mid.—What line?
End.—Clothes line, at night.

---

I got a job baking bread; the bottom fell out of the oven; there was a graveyard near, so I got a tombstone and placed it in the bottom of the oven and commenced to bake again. I got discharged next day; the customers brought the bread back and on the bottom of every loaf was, "Sacred to the Memory of Patrick Flynn."

---

## TRAVELING AGENT.

Mid.—Good evening, Mr. Wilson; how is your health this evening? You look very well.

End.—Well, dat's jist what I *isn't*. I guess I got de mumps or glanders or somethin'—I can't eat nor do nuffin, I feel so uncomformable.

Mid.—I'm sorry for that. I wanted to—

End.—Now don't talk to me; git old Tambo ober dere to conversashin wid you.

Mid.—I was merely going to ask you why a tough story is like a bier?

End.—Does you mean lager beer?

Mid.—No, nothing of the kind.

End.—Ask Tambo, den; I don't know nuffin' 'bout no udder kind ob beer.

Mid.—I'll tell you, then, why a tough story is like a *bier;* because it's a *stretcher.*

End.—Talkin' of stretchers, I was ridin' in de Hudson Ribber cars one mornin' when dere comes in a six-footed feller from down East, wid a gre-at carpet bag.

Mid.—A six-footed, fellow, sir? Impossible.

End.—Yes he did—a feller dat stood six foot in his boots, wid legs like a pair o' tongs; and spreadin' hisself out on one seat, wid his feet in anodder, says he, "Excuse me, ladies," says he "Ise a travelin' agent from Boston." And den he tucked his bag under de seat and smole upon de people like he bin eatin' a good meal. Bime-by he get tired ob de scrouchin', and went ober wid de carpet bag to anodder seat, and says he, "Excuse me, ladies, I'se a trabelin' agent from Boston," and so on, till he got kind o' sociable and 'gan to ax questions. Bime-by again, he saw a prize cow, butiful animal was dat mudderly cow; he saw him as he look troo de winder, and he ax a lady sittin' nex' to him, "What am dat?" says he. *"I think it must be a trabelin' agent from Boston, by the size of its mouf,"* says she. And dat man nebber excused himself on dat train no more.

Mid.—He must have been the original carpet bagger.

---

## PASSING COUNTERFEIT MONEY.

End.—I'm the most unfortunate man you ever saw. I get into all kinds of trouble. I saw a friend of mine fall off a car and roll in the mud. I went to him and got a stick and commenced rubbing the mud off him, when along came a policeman and arrested me.

Middle.—What for?

End.—Merely *scraping an acquaintance*. While I was in court I saw a remarkable case; a deaf and dumb man was brought in, and the judge made a remarkable cure right there.

Mid.—What was it?

End.—He gave the deaf man a *hearing*. Then a pickpocket was brought in, charged with picking pockets in a crowd. The judge fined him fifteen dollars. The pickpocket said: "Judge, all the money I've got with me is a ten dollar bill." The judge says: "All right! Give me the ten dollars." Then the judge says to the cop: "Officer, turn this man loose in the crowd and let him get me the other five dollars." As I was leaving court, I noticed a ten-dollar bill lying on the sidewalk. I stooped to pick it up, but it looked like a counterfeit bill, so I passed on.

Mid.—And the bill turned out to be a good one, of course?

End.—No; but I was arrested before I had gone a dozen steps further.

Mid.—Arrested! What for?

End.—For *passing* counterfeit money.

---

## DAMAGES.

I was at a party the other night and kissed a girl; she had me arrested and sued me for damages. She didn't get any damages out of me though, for I proved to the court she had no sign up, "look out for paint."

## CARELESSNESS.

It's wonderful how careless people are in our days. If a person walks on the street some one is bound to step on his toes and say, "excuse me;"jab an umbrella in his eye and say "excuse me" after the harm is done. The other day I saw an expressman knock a man down and run right over him with a big team, and after he ran over him the expressman hollered ''look out!'' The man looked up and said: ''Why, are you coming back?''

---

End.—Women are the ruination of men.

Mid.—You shouldn't talk of women that way. Remember, when man is sick, woman is always found at his bed-side.

End.—Yes! going through his pockets for loose change.

---

## KEPT IT UP TILL THE LAST.

Mid.—When does a young lady go into the lumber business? When she *pines* for her sweetheart, who is a *spruce* young man with *ebony* face, and of whom she thinks a great deal. Now don't say that this is a *chestnut*.

Mid.—While I remember it, I wish to call you to account. You told certain people that I was a famous liar.

End.—No; I didn't say that. I never made use of such an expression. I said you were an *infamous* liar. Speaking of liars, how's your father? There is the greatest old liar that ever lived.

Mid.—Don't dare to call my father a falsifier!

End.—He's not a falsifier, he's just a plain old liar. He'd rather lie than eat. He'd lie all the time.

Mid.—Don't speak of him in that manner; he's dead.

End.—You don't say so. What was the complaint?

Mid.—*There was no complaint.*

End.—*Everybody was satisfied, I s'pose.* Where did he die?

Mid.—He died in the house.

End.—Did he die standing up?

Mid.—Certainly not. He died *lying!*

End.—*He kept it up to the last didn't he?*

---

## ABBREVIATIONS OF STATES.

Concerning states: What is the most **religious state?** Mass.

The most egotistical? Me.

Not a state for the untidy? Wash.

The most Asiatic? Ala or Ind.

The father of states? Pa.

The most maidenly? Miss.

The most useful in haying time? **Mo.**

Best in time of flood? Ark.

Decimal state? Tenn.

State of astonishment? La.

State of exclamation? O.

State to cure the sick? Md.

The most unhealthy? Ill.

Best states for students? Conn.

State where there is no such word as fail? **Kan.**

## TWO WRONGS MAKE A RIGHT.

Two wrongs don't make a right.

Yes, it does.

How so?

Why, someone passed a counterfeit five-dollar bill on me to-day; that was wrong. I gave it to my landlady for board; that was wrong, but it made me right.

---

## HAD NO OBJECTION.

I met Mr. ———— (name someone in your city) the other day at the railroad station; he had the cheek to ask me for a chew of tobacco in presence of my two lady friends. I pulled out a plug I'd just bought, and he said: "have you got a knife?" I said: "No." Then he asked me if I had any objection where he bit it, and I said "no." He said: "all right," and jumped on the train and said: "I'll bite it in the next town."

---

## THE CIGAR TRICK.

Mid.—I attended a reception last evening and I saw a clever thing. I think I can reproduce it. It is an optical illusion. (Produces two cigars from vest and holds them up to view.) How many cigars do I hold in my hand?

End.—Two.

Mid.—You are wrong; I have three! I'll prove it. Here's one, and here's two! Two and one are three. See! It's a simple trick in addition and an optical illusion. (Is about to return cigars to vest and laughing over his cleverness.)

End.—Wait a minute. Do that again, will you? (Coaxes Mid. to show the trick again, which he does by pointing to one cigar, then to the other, then adding them.)

Mid.—Here's one, here's two. Two and one are three. Three cigars. Very clever.

End.—Let me see if I could do that.

Mid.—Oh, no! you're not clever enough.

End.—If it was too clever, you couldn't do it. Here's one, there's two. Two and one are three.

Mid.—That's it. Give me the cigars!

End.—Let me do it again? (Counts as before.) Here's one, here's two. Two and one are three. Very clever! (Two other End men.) Have a cigar? (End man takes it.) I'll keep this one. (Puts remaining cigar in his vest pocket and returns to seat.)

Mid.—Here, here! Where's my cigar?

End.—(Laughs.) You smoke the *third* one!

---

## A CIGAR WRAPPER.

I went into cigar store and bought a cigar. I bit the end off and pulled out a piece of calico. I told the proprietor I didn't come here to buy dry goods. He said: "Don't blame me; it was the fault of the girl that made it; she didn't know the difference between a Mother Hubbard and a Connecticut wrapper."

---

## IN THE SOUP.

End.—Did you know that vegetables can speak to one another?

Mid.—I was not aware of it.

End.—Oh, yes; do you know what the carrot said to the turnip when it was pulled out of the ground?

Mid.—No.

End.—I'll meet you in the soup.

---

## A BAG OF SALT.

I was walking down the street the other evening and I met Casey who keeps the grocery store; he bet me a dollar and a half that I couldn't carry a five-pound bag of salt around the corner and back again without laying it down. Well, I thought the man was a fool, but I took the bet, carried it clean around the block and came into the store and laid it on the counter. He said: "You've lost!" I said: "How so?" He said: "Didn't you just lay the bag down?" Well, I thought I'd get even on some one, so the first man I met I made him the same bet. He bet me, took the bag, carried it around the block and came into the store and hung it up on a nail. The blamed fool.

---

## MUD.

End.—What are we made from?

Mid.—The good book says we are made from dirt.

End.—Is that so? I can see now why you never take a bath.

Mid.—Why?

End.—If you do your name is mud.

## WHAT IS LOVE?

End.—What is love?

Mid.—I know what the poet says of love.

End.—What does he say?

Mid.—"Two souls but with a single thought, two hearts that beat as one."

End.—That isn't it at all.

Mid.—What is love, then?

End.—Love is a tickling sensation of the heart that cannot be scratched.

---

He is the thinnest man I ever saw. He has to wear a clapboard on his back to keep his backbone from cutting his suspenders in two.

Meanest man I ever saw, too mean to buy a collar button. He has a mole on the back of his neck and he buttons his collar on it.

---

## A SOIREE.

Mid.—Where were you going the other evening, when I saw you?

End.—Did you see me? Why, dat was *Jane Ann Forbidden Fruit*, my sweetheart. I was takin' her to the sore-eye.

Mid.—Soiree, you mean.

End.—Yes, de place where dey clinch.

Mid.—Dance, you mean.

End.—Yes; at dat ball we was de preserbed ob all de preserbers.

Mid.—Observed of all observers, you should say. I suppose you were in every set?

End.—Yes; I sot down when I went in de ball-room, and didn't get up till de ball busted up.

Mid.—I suppose you had all the principal dances?

End.—Yes; we danced de cow-choker, the poker, de landers; but dar was one dance beat any'ting you eber saw.

Mid.—What was it called?

End.—Scotch-eitch.

Mid.—No, no; you mean Schottisch.

End.—Well, I don't know, I was afraid to dance it for fear I would kotch it. Just as I was preparing to dance the redowa, in rushed a cream-colored coon, wid de big dinner-dish tied on a string, and a drum stick in his hand, and he beat dat dinner-dish wid all his might and tried to break it; but de dinner-dish was too much for him.

Mid.—No, sir; that wasn't a dinner-dish—that was a gong.

End.—Yes; dey was all gone as soon as dey heard it; and dat gal ob mine was de first one down to de table; she sat down right in front ob a big chicken; and you ought to see dat chicken after she sot dar fifteen minutes.

Mid.—Why?

End.—Why; it looked jes' like a frame house struck by lightning. 1 t'ought I would take a hack at dat chicken myself, but dat gal put herself on de outside ob de whole carcas.

Mid.—What else did you have?

End.—We had eighteen carrot vegetable soup, an' double barreled tom cat-chup, an—

Mid.—No! no! you mean tomato catsup.

End.—Yes; I know dat it was all katched up before

I got any ob it, but, I golly, dar was one dish dar—I neber saw such a dish.

Mid.—What was it called?

End.—Cold slop.

Mid.—Cold slaw, you mean.

End.—Yes; it looked like a head of cabbage, hit by a masked battery, but dat gal, she made one of de awfulest calls you eber heard ob.

Mid.—What did she call for?

End.—Why, she axed the waiter if he wouldent be so kind as to pass her up a yard ob pork.

Mid.—What an idea—a yard of pork!

End.—Yes; but she got it, though.

Mid.—How did she get a yard of pork?

End.—Don't three feet make a yard?

Mid.—Yes.

End.—Well, den, de waiter fotched her *three pig's feet.*

---

## A COLORED THEATER.

Mid.—Mr. Wilson, I notice you have taken to wearing your hair *a la* Brutus, and are giving yourself a great many airs in consequence.

End.—Yes? Well, I'll tell you all about it. You know Clem Johnson? Well, I met Clem todder night, and says Clem, says he: "Mr. Johnson, suppose we start a colored freeayter, hey? Take dem all down. Gib dem a touch ob de African Roscius. What you say." "How you do it?" says I. "We got no capital." "Why," says Clem, "we diwide de spec' into shares, like de Credit Mobilerums, and dey can buy up de stock for it." "Buy up de stock company?" said I; "and what you do wid de stars?" "O, we won't hab no *sta'rs*," said Clem; "hab it all one floor." So we fix' de 'liminaries, and de lecture room ob de chapel was turned into de freeayter, and de paster, Brudder Howler, he writ de play, and Clem made himself stage manager and said he must go and cast de company. When Clem tole us all to be ready for de 'hearse de next day dere was a rollin of eyes roun' de room, I tell you! "What for de hearse?" spokes up one big buck nigger "aint a goin' to bury us, are you?"

Mid.—It was probably the *play* that was to be damned. Your turn hadn't come yet.

End.—And when de company dissembled for de 'formance, and de colored brass band had take dair seats and was waitin' to begin, says Clem from de curtain to de leader, "Gib em de overture." "We aint got no piece by dat name, but we'll try em on "Wake snakes,"~ says de conductor. Bime-by some one cried out "Histe dat rag!" and when de prompter's bell rang, blest if half de niggars in de room didn't make a rush fo' de do!

Mid.—What was that for, sir?

End.—De force ob habit; dey tought deir missus was ringin' for dem. H'ya! h'ya! "Well, now den," says Clem to de promoter, says he, "Gib us de cue to go on." "Cue," says de prompt; "dere aint none here, but I'll send out to a billiard-saloon and git one."

Mid.—Why a *billiard* cue?

End.—To make his "points" wid, I s'pose. Den Clem look at de book, and says he, readin,' "Enter center door, flat," Wid dat he trow himself on his face and crawled in on his ear.

Mid.—Crawled in, sir. Why the "flat" means the scene, you goose!

End.—De *play* must have been flat, to judge by de way dey "goosed" it from de front. Den a brefles silence settled on de audience and dere was a blinkin' of de whites ob de eyes towards de stage. Den Clem rose up and commence:

"Down sinks de sun, and night's black pall descends—
(*Here de carpenter drap a black cloth on him from de flies.*

Brack as de deeds dat I am now to do.

De thunder roareth an' de lightning flash,
It is a nigger and a nipping air,
And now, as dat's de case, I'll take a *nip*
(*Drinkin' from his flask.*)

Hark, some one comes—
'Tis he, 'tis he, 'tis he!
Now, nerves be iron, and O, arm strike home!"

Wid dat he flourish his dagger and backs up de stage, as Pete Simcox comes on, limpin', to de slow scrapin' of de fiddles, and draggin' a lot of dried boughs along wid him; and Clem passes de cue ober to him and he commences:

"I've borne dese 'limbs' as fur as dey will go.
(*Here he frows dem down.*)

And I can't get no furder; shine out, moon,
Twinkle ye little luminous orbs of hebben
Out ob dem clouds, and light me to my lub!

Hahr! I hear footsteps. Yes—'tis she, 'tis she!"

Here Dinah Flatfoot—Dine was de hero ob de piece, you know—she rushes in and throws herself onto his bosom.

"He's found at last; now welcome, welcome death."

Mid.—What does she welcome death for when she has just found her lover?

End.—Don't know; it was in de play.

"Soft, soft!" says Pete, pattin' her on de head.

Mid—That was anything but complimentary to the lady.

End.—Dem was de words.

"Soft! if but a whisper should be heard,
  Some idle tongue the tidings might convey—"

Mid.—Why you said something about the thunder roaring and the lightning flashing. She must bellow to be heard.

End.—At dis juncture Clem comes out from behind de tree;

"Now, fortune, goddess, guide me to my prey
And steel my sinews for de damning deed!
Catiff, let go, stand off! 'tis me, 'tis me!"

Den de gal shriek an' trow her han's up to de skies, and Clem makes a plunge at Pete wid a hash knife, and she flings herself on his bosom, and de knife goes troo bofe o' dem, and dey fall ober and go into convulsions. Den Pete 'scubbers dat he hab got de wrong pussons—he wus layin' for chicken thieves in his back yard, you know, and stuck his knife into his sister and de chap dat comes courtin' her, by mistake. His feelin's is terrible; he says:

"O, ah! what hab I done? Now you, great Jove,
Launch from yon skies a bolt of biggest size
And let it on dis stupid head descend!"

Den de carpenter let fly an iron bolt at Clem's head dat nearly cove it in; an' de last I heard of Clem he was up in de skylight, peltin' it into old Gabe Haskins for nearly killing him outright wid de bolt of de scuttle. Just 'bout den de sheriff come along wid de possum-to-come-it-at-us and arrested us for playin' widout a license, an' dat bust de shop.

Mid.—It was about time you were all arrested for such murderous doings.

## THE FIRST WHITE MAN.

" 'Strate am de road an' narrow am de paff which leads off to glory!' Bredern Blevers: You am 'sembled dis night in coming to hear de word and have splained and 'monstrated to yu; yes yu is—and I tend for to splain it as de lite ob de liben day. We am all wicked sinners hea below—it's a fack, my brederen' and I tell you how it cum. You see.

> 'Adam was de fust man,·
> Ebe was de tudder,
> Cane was de wicked man
> 'Kase he kill his brudder.'

Adem and Eve were bofe brack men, and so was Cane and Abel. Now I s'pose it seems to strike yer understanding how de fust white man cum. Why, I let you know. Den you see when Cane kill his brudder de massa cum and say, 'Cane, whar's your brudder Abel?' Cane say, 'I don't know, massa.' But the nigger node all de time. Massa now git mad and cum agin; speak mighty sharp dis time. 'Cane, whar's your brudder Abel, yu nigger?' Cane now git frightened and he turn white; and dis de way de fust white man cum upon dis earth! And if it had not been for dat dar nigger Cane we'd nebber been trubbled wid de white trash 'pon de face ob dis yer circumlar globe. De quire will sing de forty-eleventh him, tickler meter. Brudder Bones pass round de sasser."

## DEAF—IN A HORN.

AN ETHIOPIAN SKETCH IN ONE ACT FOR BANJOIST AND
MOCK BANJO (''BONES.'')

### CHARACTERS.—''DEAF—IN A HORN.''

Young Orfeeus ........................Billy Birch
Plato White [A Dandy Field Hand.]

### COSTUMES.

Young Orfeeus.—Page's suit of sky blue, tight—big
bell buttons on jacket, the sleeves of which are much
too short—legs of pantaloons too short—striped stockings—ankle boots—short cross wig. He is very boyish
in his actions, and sharp and quick in speech; after
the assumed deafness is thrown off—red underjacket.

Plato.—White pantaloons, tight in the legs, and with
broad, extravagant stripes, flashy barred or flowered
waistcoat too large for him, and a large handkerchief
or muffler in the half-open bosom—bright colored cra-
vat, with loose ends, passed through a curtain ring,
where it ties—old-fashioned white beaver or wool hat,
with the nap rubbed the wrong way, worn on one side
of the head—wig, the wool rather long, and dressed
fancifully—*one* glove, white. Banjo to play. He is
very consequential, and mouths long words for effect.

### PROPERTIES.

Two chairs—mock banjo, the handle separate from
the other part—a large valise or carpet bag, to hold
the mock banjo—a large tin horn, in a bag.

### SCENE.

An Interior; door R. and L., to open and shut.—Time
of representation, ten minutes.

## DEAF—IN A HORN.

Enter Plato, L., playing on banjo, dragging a chair to L. C. front.

Plato.—Well, well, de ole house begins to look a little comfortable since de broker's man come for the tables and chairs. [*Tries if chair will bear him.* ] I'se got to be cautious ob dis furniture, 'tain't insured. [*Sits down after dusting chair with coat tail—plays a few chords un steadily.*] Dis won't do nohow. De fac' is my narvous cistern is so shaken wid de bills dat come in when I didn't hab a cent, dat the least lilly bit of sound startles me. [*About to play. Knock* R. *—jumps—looks around.*] Oh, wha—what was dat? [*Knock* R. *louder.*] Oh! come in! [*Knock* R. *much louder.*] Bimeby dey'll have de door down. [*Roars out.*] Come in. [*Knock* R. *very loud, with a kick at the same time—*Plato *jumps up.*] Guess dar's a new railroad started through my premises! [*Crosses to* R.] Co-o-me in, whoever y'are!

[Knock begins at R., when Plato opens it, and Orfeeus hit him, instead of the door.—Plato seizes Orfeeus by the collar, and drags him to C.—Orfeeus, who is holding his bag in one hand and his cap and banjo-handle in the other, falls over a chair, L. C. front, and spreads himself on stage.]

Plato.—[*Brings chair from* R. *to* C., *picks up Orfeeus, shakes him.*] I said, Come in! Why didn't you come in before? Was that you that's been a-hammering round de house all dis last week? [*Shaking him.*

[Orfeeus, while Plato shakes him, picks up his bag, etc., and looks deeply astonished at his reception.]

Plato [*Lets him go*].—Why, what ails you? You look all of a heap. [*Sits down in* L. *chair of two* C. *front.*

Plato.—You had better sit down. [*Tunes his banjo —pause—looks up.*] Sit down, I say! [*Gets up, pulls Orfeeus in front of chair, and pushes him down in it*] Now, then! [*Takes his own seat.*] What's your business? [*Orfeeus stares straight before him.*

Plato.—What's your business, I say? What do you want? [*Claps Orfeeus on the shoulder.*

[Orfeeus starts, drops his bag from right hand, and his cap and banjo from left hand.]

[*Plato's foot is hit by the banjo-handle. In a howl.*] —What—do—you—wa—a—nt?

[Orfeeus slowly bends down to his right, opens bag with large key in it, takes out horn, and applies it to his left ear—all very slowly and gravely.]

Plato [*Is amazed—then puts his mouth to horn*]—I say, what do you want here?

Orfeeus.—Yes. [*Puts horn into bag.*] I can't hear. [*Stares before him.*

Plato.—No, no! What is it you're come for? [*Slaps Orfeeus' shoulder.*

Orfeeus *starts.*

Plato [*Makes sign*].—Oh, put up that machinery of yours.

Orfeeus.—[*Same business as before, takes horn from bag and applies it to his ear.*]

Plato.—Here goes for de fog-signal! [*Mouth to horn.*] I want to know what you're come for?

Orfeeus [*Putting back the horn*].—Yes, me mudder sent me.

Plato.—Oh, your mudder sent you? Why, who's your —oh [*suddenly*] you're young Orfeeus Skeevendick, then, what's come here for to take lessons of me? Your mudder told me about you being an- intellectiligent poo-pil. [*Examines* Orfeeus.] A bright specimen of 'ornithology, I'll bet. Well, can you sing?

[Orfeeus *looking vacantly before him.*

Plato [*Impatient, nearly knocks* Orfeeus *over with a shove*]. I ask you, can you—oh, put up that trumpet ag'in!

[Orfeeus *takes horn from bag and applies it to his ear.*

Plato.—Can you sing?

Orfeeus.—Yes.

Plato.—Ah, that's better. What's your voice, high or low?

Orfeeus.—Yes, I've brought my banjo.

[*Puts horn in bag. Takes from bag the drum part of a banjo and screws handle to it.*]

Plato [*Laughs*].—Can you sing? What notes are you best on. [Orfeeus *puts horn to ear;* Plato *repeats.*]

Orfeeus.—Oh, yes. I've got my red vest on.

Plato.—No! no! Who was 'squiring 'bout your wardrobe? What's your favorites in the gamut? A, B, or C——?

Orfeeus.—Yes; D, E, F!

Plato.—I believe that much from you. [*Impatiently.*] Keep up dat horn! But how are you going to learn anythink, and can't hear a word I say?

Orfeeus.—Yes. Mudder says she ain't going to pay. Your'e to take it out in ironing and mangling.

[*Puts down horn.*

Plato.—We know all about dat. But how can you get on when you can't hear? I offen see moosical folks wid horns in deir moufs, but horns in deir ears *is* original. [*Aside, watching* Orfeeus, w*ho pays him no attention.*] But now I come to think of it—I saw dis same boy 'mong a flock of odder young kids, and he was get-

ting along pretty well. I'll try him. [*Lays his banjo*
L. *of him—aloud.*] Well, I'm sorry, Orfeeus, but I
don't think I can teach you anything. [*Rises leisurely;
—in a quiet, natural voice.*] 'Tain't no fault of your'n,
o' course, and so, as I'm gwoin' down the street,
'spose you come along and have a drink?

Orfeeus [*Jumps up quickly*].—I don't mind, thank'ee!

Plato [*Turns on him*].—Ho! ho!    [*Threateningly.*

[Orfeeus bursts into a peal of laughter, but as Plato
looks severe and advances, he lets the laugh die away
and retreats to R. front.]

Plato ([*Follows* Orfeeus *to* R.*—savagely*].—How dare
you play such a trick on a genbleman?

Orfeeus [*Looking around*].—I don't see no genbleman!

Plato [*Drags* Orfeeus *to* C.].—I've a good mind to
pull your ears!

Orfeeus.—Don't! Your'n looks if you'd got perfec'
in practice!

[*Makes a sudden dive for his cap, but* Plato *brings
down his foot near it, and* Orfeeus *pretends he did not
mean to pick it up.*]

Plato.—Come, now, will you behove yourself, and take
your lessons properly, if I let you off dis time?

[*Seated as before.*

Orfeeus.—Oh, yes! sartin true, black and blue!
[*Takes seat as before.*] Ha! ha! I knew I could fool
ye!

Plato [*Playing banjo*].—No more foolin', anyhow.
Do you know the scale?

Orfeeus.—Yes. Lots of 'em at the fishmonger's!

Plato.—I don't mean that! Can you run the gamut?

Orfeeus.—Oh, yes, unless he's too fast for me.

Plato [*Vexed*].—What's your compass?

Orfeeus.—I ain't got no compass. De ole man has, though; he's a *merino*.

Plato.—A what?

Orfeeus.—A merino—on a coal barge!

Plato.—Oh, a mariner. I don't mean a sailor's compass.

Orfeeus.—Oh!

Plato.—I mean the compass of your voice. Are your notes in your chest good?

Orfeeus.—I on'y had one note in my chest, and that's so bad that thieves won't take it.

[*Pretending to tune his mock banjo.*

Plato [*Stopping his pretended tuning*].—I ain't talking the money article. Let's hear you sing.

Orfeeus.—Hem! hem! What'll I sing?

Plato.—Oh! anything you like.

Orfeeus [*Shakes his head*].—I used to know ''Something to Love,'' but I never heer'd on ''Anything You Like.''

Plato.—Well, I'll start you. [*Chord or two.*] All you've got to do is join in the chorus.

[Orfeeus *pretends to play very extravagantly.* Plato *plays and sings.*]

### SALLY IS THE GAL FOR ME!

When I am in the weaving way
I spends my money free,
I makes the cash and cuts the dash—
Oh, Sally is the gal for me!
*Chorus.*
Oh, Sally is the gal for me!

Plato [*Repeats chorus; then.*]—Why don't you come in?

[Orfeeus *turns in his chair and looks toward door.*

Plato.· Why don't you come in?

Orfeeus.—I didn't hear nobody knock.

Plato.—Knock?—who?—what?

Orfeeus.—You just tol' somebody to come in!

Plato.—Get out. [Orfeeus *rises*.] Sit down! [*Moves* Orfeeus' *chair*.]

[Orfeuss *falls in sitting, and, in falling, kicks away* Plato's *chair—Plato has half risen, laughing, when, in sitting down, he falls. Picture of the two sitting on the floor beside one another, looking at one another.*]

Plato [*Gets up*].—Why, what's up?

Orfeeus [*Rising*].—I was till you pulled me down!

Plato.—Who told you to leff your chair?

Orfeeus.—You—you told· me to get out! [*Picks up his banjo and resumes his seat—examines his banjo.*] I mos' think dar's some ob de bones broke.

Plato [*Tuning up*].—I mean—now, look y'ah! All got to do is to come in on de chorus. I say, "Cuts a dash!"—you say, "Oh, Sally is de Gal for Me!" first time. Nex' time you repeat it twice't—d'you see?

Orfeeus.—Oh, yes; I see. "Sally is de Gal for Me!" [*Laughs. Plato plays and sings as before. At "Cuts a dash!" Orfeeus, who has been pretending to play all the time, shouts out:* "Oh, Sally is de Gal for Me, first time!"] [*Playing.*

[Plato, *at the end of his patience, pushes* Orfeeus *sideways. Orfeeus falls, striking the floor loudly with his banjo, to break it. Plato throws his chair over on* Orfeeus, *and piles two others on him.*]
[*Exit* L.

Orfeeus [*Rises slowly and picks up his bag, banjo, etc. Then, pointing to the chairs, laughs.*]—I guess—guess-y-guess it's all right! I got three *cheers*, anyhow. [*Exit* R.

## THE BET.

"Pompey, I saw your schoolmaster yesterday; he says you're getting along like a house a-fire.

"Yes, I've been to a *cemetery* for my edification."

"To a cemetery? Pray, how long have you been dead?"

"I didn't say I was dead, although I studied some in de dead languages. I mean to say I've been to a *cemetery*—a schoolhouse—a scolledge."

"Ah! I see. You mean a seminary, Pompey."

"Yes, a Seminaw."

"You're a very good speller, I hear."

"Yes, as to dat, I can spell anything, Sam."

"You can, eh?"

"Yes, indeed, Sam. I beat all de boys at reduction-multiplication, addition, substraction, and when it comes down to spelling! Well, go 'way, I'm dar, Sam."

"Well, now, Pompey, let me hear you spell '*Weather.*' "

"Oh! I can't spell dat, but I'll try. Weather; what, de weather dat's caused by the firmamence?"

"Yes; go on, sir."

"Wh—th—ch—er, weather—ly—lee!"

"Weel, that's the worst spell of weather we've had for a long time."

"You don't like it? Well, if you don't have no worse spell of weather than dat, it's well for you dat de equinoctial is passed over. I could spell hog better dan dat."

"Why, you can't spell anything, Pompey. You can't spell *coffee-pot* without saying *tea-pot*."

"I can't, Sam?"

"No, I *know* you can't.

"You *know* I can't? Dat's a broad assertion."

"Well, I'll back it.

"What'll you bet?"

"Five dollars."

"You bet five dollars dat I can't spell *coffee-pot* widout sayin' *tea-pot?*"

"Yes."

"Put up your money. Now, I'll bet five, ten, fifteen, twenty, twenty-five—well, say thirty, forty, fifty, sixty, seventy, eighty, ninety—say a hundred?"

"Very well; a hundred it is."

"Well, I guess you'd better make it a dollar."

"Very well, then; one dollar."

"Well, professor, I don't think I've got a dollar about me; won't you trust? I'll tell you what I'll do —I'll bet my suit of clothes agin your suit of clothes?"

"Very well, sir; go on."

"C-o-f-f-e-e—coffee, *p-o-t*, *pot*."

"Dere, you've lost, Pompey; you said 'tea-pot.' "

"Yes, I know I did; well, you'll give me a chance to get even, won't you, professor? [*Putting his hands in his pockets.*] I'll bet you anoder suit of clothes dat I ain't got my hands in my pockets."

"Well, that's a very foolish bet."

"Well, you take it, dat's all."

"Well, come, I won't be dared. I do take it. Ha! ha! ha! [*Laughs heartily.*] I've won again, for you've got your hands in your pockets now."

"These ain't *my pockets*."

"Why not?"

"*Didn't you just win dese clothes,* Sa-ay?"

## ROUGH ON TAMBO.

Interlocutor.—How are you getting along these hard times, Mr. Bones?"

Bones.—*I'm* gettin' along all right, but dey say old Tambo hain't paid his washwoman dese free months."

Int.—How's that, Tambo—is luck so hard against you as that?

Tabo.—Dat report is a untroof. I hain't *had* no washin' done dese free months, darfore I don't owe nuffin'.

---

## YOU BET!

"Pete, I wish you to answer me a question."

"What is it, Eph?"

"Do you know who is the greatest man in the world?"

"Yes, sir, I do."

"Who?"

"Uncle Sam."

"Why so?"

"'Cause he's de champion game cock ob liberty."

"Is he great in any other way?"

"Yes-sir-ee."

"In what manner?"

"Why, he's de fearless and unconquerable hero ob de world."

"Is he married?"

"Who, Uncle Sam?"

"Yes."

"Of course he is."

"And to whom?"

"Miss Columbia was married to him."

"Have they any offspring?"

"Yes-sir-ee."

"How many?"

"Thirty-nine yungun's."

"Who and what are they?"

"Dese glorious United States ob 'Merica."

---

### THE BLACK SWAN.

"Lem, I went out de oder night and slammanded de Black Swine."

"No, no; you mean you serenaded the Black Swan."

"Yes—we went dar, 'bout twenty-seben ob us, got underneaf de winder, and commenced playin' dat soul-stirring melody ob——

"'Beats dere a heart, beat dere a heart,
　　On earf, on earf, sincere——'
She 'spected us."

"She did?"

"Yes, sir; fur all at once de winder went up, de shutters flew back, and she herself—individually—came forth in all her sylph-like beauty and dishibilly, wid her hair all dressed up pooty in little gimlets."

"Ringlets, you intended to say."

"Yes, she poked her head out ob de winder, and says, 'Gem'len, how many is dere ob you?' I told her 'leben or eight; she den said: 'Take dis and divide it between you,' and wid her own hand she threw——'

"What?"

"De contents ob a slop-pail all ober us. She told us to come 'round de next night and she'd be ready to——'

"What?"

"Scald us."

## STUMP SPEECH.
### "GO WORK FOR YOUR LIBIN'.!"

"My tex, bruderen and sistern, will be found in de fus' chapter ob Ginesis, and de twenty-seben verse: 'So de Lor' made man jus' like Hese'f.' Now, my bruderen, you see dat in de beginnin' ob de world de Lor' made Adam. I tole you how he make him: He make 'im out ob clay, an' he sot 'im on a board, an' he look at him, an' he say 'Firs' rate'; and when he get dry he breathe in 'im de breaf ob life. He put him in de Garden of Eden, and he sot 'im in one corner ob de lot, an' he tole him to eat all de apples, 'ceptin' dem in de middle ob de orchard; dem he wanted for he winter apples. Bymebye Adam he got lonesome. So de Lor' make Ebe. I tole you how he make her: He gib Adam lodlum, till he get sound 'sleep; den he gouge a rib out he side and make Ebe; and he set Ebe in de corner ob de garden; an' he tole her to eat all de apples, 'ceptin' dem in de middle ob de orchard; dem he winter apples. Wun day de Lor' go out a bisitin'; de debbil come along; he dress hisself in de skin ob de snake, and he find Ebe; an' he tole her: 'Ebe, why for you no eat de apple in de middle ob de orchard?' 'Ebe say: 'Dem de Lor's winter apples.' But de debbil say: 'I tole you for to eat dem, case dey's de best apples in de orchard.' So Ebe eat de apple an gib Adam a bite; an' de debbil go away. Bymebye de Lor' come home, an' he miss de winter apples; an' he call: 'Adam! you Adam!' Adam he lay low; so de Lor' call again: 'You, Adam!' Adam say: 'Hea, Lor'!' And de Lor' say: 'Who stole de winter apples?' Adam tole him he don't know—Ebe, he expec'! So de Lor' say: 'Ebe!' Ebe she lay low; de Lor' call again: 'You Ebe!' Ebe say: Hea, Lor'!' De Lor' say: 'Who stole de winter apples?' Ebe tole him she don't know—Adam, she expec'! So de Lor' cotch 'em boff, and de throw dem over de fence, an' he tole em: 'Go work for your libin'!'"

---

## ONE GAL EQUAL TO FOUR QUARTS.

When you come to think of it, the old folks used to by the schemes; but it's different now. The young folks are the ones now; the young folks can give the old ones pointers on most everything. They can beat them at their own game. Now, for example, we will take the theater right here. Now when the young folks come they come in pairs. Now, what I mean by pairs is this: The young lady, two or three days before she wants to go to the theater, always picks out the softest cake she's got on her string (of course present company excepted), and when they sit down watch them closely. Just notice how he'll be deeply interested in every little item that takes place on this stage. Not so with her. She's sitting there figuring on how she's going to work him for the ice cream after the show. Then, when the show is over and they get out on the sidewalk, you'll notice the first thing she does is to throw her head way up, while he will be looking across the street. You might think that with her head up there she was enjoying the beautiful evening. Not so; she's looking for signs where it says, "Ice Cream." He's looking for signs, too, but not those kind of signs. He's looking for signs where it says, "Schooners *(that high)* for five, and lunch throwed in.'' Finally, after a nice little bit of strategy, she lands him into this ice cream parlor. Down they sit, up comes the waiter; she asks first, ''What kind have you got?'' The waiter says, ''We've got vanilla, strawberry——'' ''Stop where you are; bring me vanilla and strawberry, but bring them separate'' (working two plates on you at once).

When the waiter starts off to fill the order, she unties her bonnet strings, throws open her wraps, and says, ''Charlie, it's awful warm here.'' (It ain't warm a bit; she's getting ready for that ice cream.) Back comes the waiter and puts the order on the table; she puts her fan up alongside of her face and coughs (that's a bluff cough); she sticks that fan up alongside her cheek in order to get a chance to sneak that chewing-gum out of her mouth and stick it under the table.

Do you know that I often wondered how it was that a young girl could get away with so much ice cream in such a short time? It interested me so much that I went through the American Encyclopædia. I failed to find it there, and I finally landed in our ordinary primary arithmetic, and there in the arithmetic the whole secret it told:—''One gal. equal to four quarts.''

---

## WILL MY CHILDREN BE GRASSHOPPERS?

Ladies, get ready for a terrible shock; I am going to surprise you. It makes me perspire when I think what I've got to tell, but it has got to be done; so here goes. I am married. (You see, I was out of work and I couldn't find anything to do, so I got married.)  But *I* had a good excuse for marrying; I was blind when *I* got married.  You know the old saying, "Love is blind."  Well, that was the case with me.  But let me tell you right here that marriage is an eye-opener.  You wouldn't believe it, but I live like a bird; I've got to fly for my life.  When a man is in love he feels his heart go right out from him, and after he is married he feels his pocket-book going right out from him.

I must tell you about my visit to Chicago.  The first two or three days I was in Chicago I got along all right; but when Saturday night came, after I got my salary (my wages), I generally got a limp in my left leg.  Me and my limp were going up State Street and somehow I imagined the street was too narrow for me, and I met a policeman; he was the most polite man I ever met.  He saw I had my limp with me and he invited me to take a ride.  I told him I didn't mind, and he went to the corner of the street and opened one of those round boxes and touched a button and up came one of the handsomest wagons I ever saw: painted and varnished to the queen's taste—prettiest wagon I ever saw.  In fact, I was carried away with it (me and my limp).  When I got out I made up my mind I would visit the town good (and leave my limp at home).  I visited all the points of interest.  I saw the Masonic Temple (twenty-two stories high), and I went through the Grand Union Hotel (I got three canes, a hat and an umbrella out of it).  After that I visited the Widows' Home.  I got acquainted with one of them and three days after that I saw her home and she sued me for breach of promise.  And that ain't the worst of it: The next day I saw her sister home and she sued me for breach of promise, too. Now, you would naturally think I had two suits, but such is not the case; I just got a pair of breaches (breeches), that's all. There is a peculiar thing about my marriage. When I married my wife was a grass-widow and I was a grass-widower. Now the question arises: If my wife was a grass-widow and I was a grass-widower, will our children be grasshoppers?

## THE HEN HAD THE GRIP.

Ladies and gentlemen, I am sorry I couldn't get here any later, but what made me late was this: I live with my brother out in the country and he keeps chickens; one of his setting hens flew off the eggs and I had to sit on them until the hen came back; and you wouldn't believe it, the minute I stepped in that chicken coop one of the hens spoke. She said, ''There is the fellow we are laying for.'' Well, to tell the truth, I have been in the habit of stealing eggs on the quiet in my brother's coop; but one day I was watched, and just as I came out of the 'coop I was struck by an egg, and the egg I was struck with was antedeluvian; it had been laying in the nest for a long time and it was covered with feathers. The minute it struck me I knew it was broke, for I never saw the atmosphere dislocated so quickly in all my life. I never thought an egg could spread so much before. The egg might have been all right, but the hen that laid it must have had a terrible case of the grip.

## I HAVEN'T GOT THE NERVE.

It's no use talking; I came from an unlucky family.
Now, my brother Bill—that is, he's my half-brother
on my mother's side—has one awful failing, and that
is, he cannot tell the truth. I have seen him struggle
very hard to tell the truth, yet he'd always wind up
with a lie. There was only one thing that kept people
from calling Bill a bare-faced liar—he had whiskers.
Now, I've got a brother Joe; he's my full brother on
my sister's side, but Bill, he's only my half-full
brother. Joe's name is very apropos of our relation-
ship, for he's full all the time. Now, Joe's great failing is to become a physician, but he has no patience
(patients). You know it requires patience (patients)
to become a physician. Now, as to myself, my great
failing was, I wanted to marry everyone I knew.

Oh! love is a peculiar thing. Now, some people
don't know what love is, but I will tell you what love
is: Love is a tickling sensation of the heart that cannot be scratched. The last family I married into is
one of the first families of Philadelphia as you come
up Lombard Street. *(Name any street where the most
colored people live.)* I tell you, when a man is in love,
he feels his heart going right out from him, and when
he's been married a short time he feels his *pocket-book*
going from him. Since I have been married not one
of the family has done any work but myself and a bottle
of catsup; the catsup worked yesterday. My mother-
in-law said to me a few days after I was married: "I
suppose you know when you married my daughter you
married the whole family." I told her I didn't know
it before I got married, but I know it now. It's nice

to be married and have a nice home and a nice little wife, a pug dog and a mother-in-law. I've got the nicest pug dog—I mean mother-in-law. Of the two I prefer the dog, because a dog will mind his own business, and so will your mother-in-law, and everyone else's business, too.

But my mother-in-law's great peculiarity was her cooking. I had two of her favorite dishes: hot tongue and cold shoulder. I have them quite often, I assure you. If there is anything she prided herself on, it was her pies. The pies she made were what you might call affectionate pies. Now, affectionate pie is where the upper crust is dead stuck on the lower. There is no room for animosity between them. I set my two back teeth in one of her pies and they are there yet. I told her one day I didn't think her pies were up to the standard and she sneered at me. Did you ever have your mother-in-law sneer at you? The minute she does, that's the time to pack your trunk and get out. Well, after she sneered, she said: ''I want you to know one thing: I made pies before you were born.'' That must have been one of the pies I got hold of. Now, at meal time, I always sit aside of ma—I always called my mother-in-law ''ma''—(I called her other names, too, but I never let her hear me).

Now, talking about appetite, I've seen my mother-in-law without money many times, but I never saw her without her appetite. Right beside ma's plate was a whole spring chicken, and would you believe it, she ate that entire chicken without offering a bite to anyone. All at once she struck a bone in the meat, so to speak, and she tried to speak, but she couldn't. I really hoped she'd choke to death—I mean I really thought she'd choke. Now, my wife always had her presence of mind. Well, that's all she's got now, for I've mortgaged everything else. My wife suggested we should send for the doctor. When the doctor came, I said: "Well, Doc.—" (I always called him Doc., for if you say Doctor, it's four dollars in advance; if you say Doc., it's two, and you can stand him off). So I said: "Well, Doc., what do you think of the case?" He looked ma right in the face. (She's got one of those open faces that you can look right into.) After looking he said: "This is a tough case." Anyone who has ever seen my mother-in-law knows she was a tough case. But I Said: "Doc., what I want to know is: do you think she will pull through?" The doctor said: "The only sure thing for your mother-in-law is to send her to a warmer climate some place where it is warm." I suggested Florida. He said: "No; that was not warm enough." So I went out into the woodshed and got the axe, and said: "Doc., you hit her; I haven't got the nerve."

---

## A SILLY COUNTRY CHAP.

I have been working in the country for five years and I saved twenty-five dollars (and a little over). I just came in town to get a birthday present for my aunt. I went into a bird store with the twenty-five dollars (and the over in my pocket). The store was chuck full of birds, parrots, *more-cheese-cats* and little dogs. There was a dog there all covered with little black spots (chuck full on the outside of the dog—*coach dog*). Oh, I tell you, he was a lal-lah! I gave the man the twenty-fi ? ollars and he gave me the dog. (I had the over

in my pocket yet.) I took the dog out by a string.
I didn't have the twenty-five dollars then; the man had
it (but I had the over and the dog). It wasn't much
of a dog for twenty-five dollars, but the man said if I
fed him good, in course of time I'd have twenty-five
dollars worth of dog. As I was taking him home, it
commenced to rain and it rained all over that poor little
dog and washed all the spots off him. I was so mad I
could hit that man; I could hit him in church. I just
thought I'd go back to the store, and if that man didn't
do something about them there spots there would be
trouble. I picked up a big rock and put it in my pocket. I was mad, I was, and I was determined if that
man didn't do something about that dog, I'd just take
that rock and haul off—and kill a parrot or something.
But the man meant well enough, for the minute he saw
me and the dog, he hollered out to his clerk: "John,
why didn't you give that man an umbrella? Here you
go, sir; an umbrella goes with that dog. (*Select a suitable song.*)

---

## A SHORT TALK BY CHARLIE CASE.

The first time I ever sang a sad ballad, was this afternoon. I didn't know how it would go, so I asked the
stage-manager to stand in the wings and tell me if it
would do. So he did. He said: "That'll do." In fact,
I had just about reached the third line, when he said:
"That'll do." It was an awful sad song. It was so
sad that a man in the audience tried to commit suicide
while I was singing it. He shot at himself twice, but he
missed himself and the bullets came right at my head.

I saw an advertisement from Weber & Fields the other

day, saying that they wanted a good act to close the show. So I asked Mr. Proctor if he would recommend me and he said that he would. He gave me a letter to Weber & Fields and it reads like this: ''I can recommend Charlie Case to you. If you want your show to close, hire him.''

If there's any place in the world I like it's California. And the people there liked me. They said they wished I would stay forever. When I got ready to go away, the paper printed the following notice about me: ''Charlie Case closed his engagement at the Orpheum theater last night and leaves for the East to-day. We would like to have him stay forever.'' They liked my father there, too. Father was only there a few months and they thought so much of him that they tried to have him settle there. In fact, for a long time after my father left, he used to get letters asking him to come back and settle.

I was engaged to a young lady once and I thought I'd tell her about it. I was engaged to her, but she didn't know it. You see, the way I knew about it was this: A fortune teller said that she was indifferent to me, and I knew right away it was Miss Thompson for I had spoken to her several times on the street and she never took any notice of me. Well, one day I saw her at the circus and I thought I'd propose to her. The circus was crowded and I had to stand up, but from where I stood I could see almost as well as if I was inside the tent. Well, I asked her if she'd marry me, and she said she wouldn't wipe her old shoes on me. I saw I had her, so I thought I'd speak to her father. I told him that I had spoken to his daughter and that she had said that she wouldn't wipe her old shoes on me. ''Well,'' said he, ''I'll wipe

mine on you.'' So I started to run up an alley. It was
so dark I couldn't see two feet ahead of me. But I saw
one foot behind me. I couldn't locate it only every once
in a while. Then I'd say, ''there it is now!''

Now you know my father is a very curious man. He's
always looking for information. If he sees anything in
the street he always wants to stoop and examine it,—
tobacco, or anything. Well, one night we were coming
home in the dark and we made a cross-cut through a
neighbor's yard, and father stooped down and picked up
something, and when we got home, where it was light
and we could examine it, we saw it was an armful of
wood. Well, this neighbor had been losing a good deal
of wood and he accused father of stealing it. As if
father would steal his wood when we had a cellar half
full of it.

You know my brother Hank and I slept in the next
room to father, and there was only a thin partition between. Well, one night after father thought he heard
burglars in the house, so he rapped on the partition and
said, ''Boys, I think there are burglars in the house, go
downstairs and see if you can find them.'' I said:
''Father's speaking to you, Hank,'' but Hank said he
hadn't lost any burglars and for me to go down and find
them. Well, Hank and I finally went down, but we
couldn't find any burglars, so we went down to the
police station and I told the police that there were
thieves in our house, and they said, ''Yes, we've been
onto it for some time.'' The police told us to go back
home and when we got there the thieves would be there.

Now my brother Hank was arrested once, and everybody thought it was funny because father was so honest.
Folks said that father was as honest as the sun. Father

used to tell us stories about his killing panthers out in the Rocky Mountains. I never disagreed with father. Hank disputed him once and lost two teeth and so I always believed everything he said. Well, father used to kill a panther every five minutes, and the way he used to kill them was this: He used to grab the panther by the tail and head and break his spine. Well, one day father and I were out in the woods and we discovered a panther 10 feet long. His front teeth were out, but some of them were only out about five or six inches; so, when father saw it he said, ''is it a horse?'' and I said ''no, it's a panther. Now you break his spine, father.'' But father said, ''no, it may belong to some poor man's family, and I'm not going to do it.'' I said, ''that don't make any difference, you break his spine and I'll go home and tell mother to start a fire to cook him.'' ''No,'' said father, ''I'll go and tell her just how I want him cooked and I see it's going to rain and I'm going to run.''

My brother Hank and I joined a theatrical company once, and we had to sing a song. When we got through, the audience made an awful racket and I asked the stage-manager if they wanted us back. ''Yes, back here,'' said he. Well, when the show was over the manager said to us, that a large portion of the audience was waiting for us at the stage door with clubs. So, Hank says to me, ''if we go sneaking down there they'll think we are afraid of them, so we'll just walk boldly out this side window.'' When we got to the depot I sent Hank out to get enough cigars to last us on the trip. In a little while he came back with both hands full—a quarter a piece. One of them was nearly whole. Hank is a good judge of cigars, although nobody every told him anything about it. He just picked it up, himself.

One day my father decided that he wanted to buy a dog. So he went to a dog fancier, and the dog fancier explained to him about the different breeds, the setter, the pointer, the Newfoundland, the St. Bernard, and in fact the whole nine breeds, and told him that every one of the nine breeds was worth $100. Well, father bought a dog from a tramp for five dollars, and from what the dog fancier had told him about the value of every breed I knew the minute I saw him that this dog was worth $900. Well, I thought I would teach the dog some tricks so I held my foot up and told him to jump over it. He seemed to catch on right away. Well, father saw he was a bright dog so he took him out in the yard to teach him some more tricks. When I came out, father was hanging onto the limb of a tree and the dog stood under him with his mouth open, ready to catch father and break his fall in case he happened to let go. I said to father, "you're getting along splendidly with him, he can walk on his hind legs already." I knew the dog had a good pedigree because I heard father explaining it to him while he was hanging by the limb.

—CHARLIE CASE.

## IMPULSIVE ORATION!

FELLER CITIZENS AND HUMANS:—Lend me your ears, for I am about to let her slide. Dis am a great country, full ob toil and troubles, sin and sorrow, sickness and deff. We spring up like a hopper-grass and are cut down like a peppergrass, as Speelshake says in his works ob human ewents. I tell yer, feller citizens, a. crisis hab aribben and sumthin's bust; our hy-per-bol-i-cal and

majestic uniwerse ob creation hab unshipped her rudder
and de captin's ded drunk in dat renowned and neber to
be forgotten place called de odder side ob Jordan; de
chambermaid hab jumped overboard and dive down to de
depths ob de mighty deep in serch ob crabs and odder
small insects.  Our wigwams am torn to pieces like an
old shirt on a brush fence.

We hab purloined de huntin' grounds ob de poor abo-
rigines, and druv dem in desperation to de plains ob
Caucassus on de Kentuck ribber, near Skeedunk Territory.

Dis am a time to be looked up to like a bobtail shanghai on a rickety henroost; am such tings to be did?  I ax
you in de name ob dat proud majestic bird ob Liberty,
which hab smelt de smoke ob many hard fought battles,
and hab now flown ober de cloud capt summits ob de
Rockygany Mountins, and sets perched on de staff ob de
Star Spangled Smasher, am such things gwine to be con-
glomerated?  Oh answer me, somebody! and ''let me
not bust wid ignorance,'' as Cæsar said when Gimblet
stabbed him in de house ob Rep re-sent-a-tives.

I'se sprung a leak! I'm spilen! I'm gwine to let her
rip, and yelp like a hungry bar wid a sore head, or a big
yaller dog wid a wheel barrow tied to his tail.

Den flock togedder, feller humans, like a flock ob tur-
key buzzards round der carcass ob a defunct mule, or a
drove ob shad in fly time, and rib me out wid a mill
grab, if I don't stick to you like brick dust to a bar ob
soft soap, or a lot ob hungry niggers to a bowl ob clam
soup.  Times aint as dey used to was, and things in
general hab got to cum to a stop, so my friend Jeems
says, and what he says am ile from de can.  Howsum-
ever, his absence prevents his hemispherical orgunnisa-
tional optical illusional powers.

Look to it, feller humans, or I will, for I am spilin'.
I'm worried and dere will be trouble in de house, and
when I do rise up, de whole Yankee nation from de East
to de Wes', from de North to de South, will exclaim in
de loud and terrific, sublime and unnatural language as
Paul de Soap Fat Man used when preachin' in de wilder-
ness to the aborgines ob Hosh Kosh, when he said unto
dem "you dat am last shall be fust, and you dat am
fust shall be last, and follow in de footsteps of de od-
ders," when Gabriel blows his horn or stay behind till
the day ob Jug-her-not and *Root little Hog or die.*

## PRESIDENCY ON THE BRAIN.

FELLER CITIZENS! !—Correspondin' to your unani-
mous call, I shall not be de undertaker to an address
you, and confine myself to de points and confluence to
which I am annihilated. Feller citizens! dis is a day to
be lookin up, like a bobtailed hen on a ricketty henroost. Somefin' has bust!

Whar is we? I am here, and am goin' to stand here
till I take root, if you'll only shout aloud and cast your
vote for your humble servant. Jee-ru-se-lem is to pay,
and we aint got no pitch.

Our patriotic canal boat ob creation has unshipped
her rudder, de captin's broke his neck, and de cook has
gone to de vasty deep in search obb diamonds. Our wigwams are torn to pieces and scattered like a shirt on a
brushy fence. Are sich things going to be did? I ask
in de name ob de shaggy-headed eagle, are such tings
going to be conflumniated? I repeat to you in de name
ob de Rockygany Mountains, are we goin' to be extra-

neously bigoted in dis fashion? Oh, answer me, as Shakspeal says:

"Do not let me blush in ignorance."

Feller Citizens and Colleagues! you have called upon me to acknowledge de inwitation as a nominee for me to de candydate to de Presidence ob dese Uncle Sam's domitory at de White House situated in dis our glorious Unicorn; and I tink if I am elected by you, it'll be "buly for me!"

And now, feller constituents, if yer elect me to be Presidens, de fust ting I'll do is to 'bolish all de toll gates and ebery man dat has to work fur a libin' shall hab instead of a dollar a day, eight York shillin's. And jest as sartin as I'm 'lected, I'll pave the streets with pancakes, and all de gutters shall run wid milk and sugar.

I'll pull down de taxes, I will—yes, sir—won't I—you'll see. And den ebery ting'll be cheaper.

I'll now git down from de high hoss dat I am on, and make room for some oder lunk-head, hopin' to see you all at de polls on 'lection day, whar you'll find a fresh watter million cub. I wish you a werry good ebenin'.

---

## MOSQUITOES.

"Sam, are you troubled werry much wid mosquitoes?"

"Yes, very much."

"So am I."

"Why, I thought you had none at all at your house."

"Oh, yes, sir, we hab all the luxuries when dey are in season, down to our domicile."

"And do they trouble you much?"

"No; but dey set one family in our neighborhood feeling very bad."

"How so?"

"Why, Sam, dey was so thick down dar last week dat dey took Bill Smith's little child ten months old right away, and nofin' haint been heard ob it since."

"And tell me how you escape from them?"

"You see, Sam, dar's only one set dat comes to my house, and I have fixed dem so dat dey can't bite any more."

"How's dat?"

"*I pulled all deir teeth.*"

---

## A MANAGER IN A FIX.

*Enter the* MANAGER *surrounded by* THE BURNT CORK BROTHERHOOD *all gesticulating and talking at once.*

Manager.—But, gentlemen, will you listen to me? You must be aware that I cannot satisfy all your demands at once. After so many years of pleasant intercourse, to be threatened with a rupture in the very moment of a managerial crisis, too! Come, be magnanimous.

Bones.—Dis 'ere ting's played out—it's *aus gespielt.* As long as dem opera chaps stuck to chalk faces and Italian, it was all werry well; but now they's takin' to burnt cork, dere's got to be a stop put to it.

Man.—Very well, sir, what would you have *me* do about it?

Tambo.—Raise our salaries and we'll howl dem down —dat's what.

Man.—Why, the new aspirants make no pretensions to the bones, that I'm aware, and I'm sure jigs and breakdowns are not in their line.

Bones.—Dat's what it's comin' to. But don't you be uneasy. Just gib us de same salaries, and if we don't shut 'em up, den my name isn't Bones.

Tambo.—Talk up to him, Bonesey—we'll back you.

Man.—Suppose I should accede to your demands, what next do you propose?

Bones.—Fight dem wid deir own weapons. Look at dat!

*(Unrolls an immense scroll of manuscript along the stage front.)*

Man.—And what may you call that, sir?

Bones.—Dat? You don't know what dat is? Well, you *am* green. Why, dat's an operum.

Man.—An opera? And what do you propose to do with it?

Bones.—Why, to perform it, to be su'. But hold on, I'll read it to you.

Man.—What! that interminable pile of rubbish! Now it's my turn to ask you to pay *me*.        *(Going.*

Bones.—Well, den, I'll compromise by singing you one scene of it, and when you've heerd it, you won't go till you've heerd all de rest.

Man.—It seems I am fated to undergo martyrdom in some shape. Proceed.

Bones.—De operum am called *Bassanola Bonum-Strike!*

Man.—That's original anyhow. Copyright, of course?

Bones.—Of course de copy's all right. Now den—de great scenes—Backyard ob de Castle of Bassalona—time midnight. Enter Baron De Harrico, with a trombone in a brown study.

Man.—A strange sort of an instrument that. But what is he going to do with a trombone?

Bones.—Goin' to lemonade his lady-lub, of course.

Man.—To serenade his lady-love with a trombone. Preposterous!

Bones.—*Am* it prepos'ous? Just listen *(Takes trombone and gives a terrible blast.)* Dat's to wake her up, you know. Den de Baron sings a sentimental song, accompanying himself on de trombone.

Man.—O, come, come, sir; how can he do that?

Bones.—Sings a line, den plays de 'companiment, and so on. Hear de song:

O, de treetoad croak in de old gum tree,
De nightowl sounds his tender lay;
Fling up your casement, listen unto me,
Don't you hear de music play.

Man.—Nonsense, sir! Treetoads and nightowls in a sentimental ballad?

Bones.—I tought I'd be 'riginal. Eb'rybody introduces de nightingale. Well, h'ya. De gal comes to de winder wid a sheet of music in her hand and a linen sheet wrapt 'round her. And she sings a duet.

Man.—Poh, sir! You mean a quartette. As well to be right while you're about it.

Bones.—Well, she pipes up wid a piccolo for de 'compayment:

O, who dat sawin' wood down dere?
You'd better make tracks or dere'll be a flare;
When de ole man's mad hear him cuss and swear,
His bosom's rage revealing.

Don Harrico:

O, hold your slack my lub, it's me;
Call sawin' wood dis harmony?

Come down and wid your lover tlee,
Here in de shadows stealing.
Now de oder lubber he comes sneakin' round; he took
de trombone for de cow, and didn't mistrust, you see.
And he sings a concertina to de flute obligato:
Tambo *sings*:

I cannot rest when true love calls,
And here my dismal plaint I pour,
The sound shall pierce her father's halls—
Hark, hark! methinks I hear her snore!

Man.—Poetic, certainly. Well, go on.
Bones.—Den Harrico gives a fearful blast on de trombone, and says he:

What tief aroun' de henroost sneaks
Dis time o' night and mischief seeks?
It am de hour when villains prowl—
Git up and git, or I'll make you howl!

Tambo, *as de oder lubber*, Harrico:
My sword's in its scabbard, my hand's on the hilt,
O, why'm I selected your blood to have spilt?
Bones.—Well, den de oder feller he lams it
into Harrico, who defen's himself wid de trombone, and
day had it lively for a few minutes, two up and two
down, and de ole man—dat's de Baron de Bassalona—
he rushes down between, and one feller run his sword
tro him and de oder knocks him down wid de trombone,
and de gal she rushes in wid a carvin' knife and slaps
it into both of dem; and when dey's all had deir las'
squall, she ups and sings a *sostenuto*, and keels over and
dies too. Den, to show it was only in fun, dey all get
up and dance a jig, and dat winds up de 'formance.
Man.—If such an astonishing production don't kill
the audience you're lucky. Let us now have something
of a different order.

## HARD TIMES.

**SERMON DELIVERED BY THE REV. JACOBUS SNOWBALL.**

Dear Grumblers:—In 'cordance wid my promise, I will spoke to you dis ebenin' on de perwailin' epidemic ob de day. You will find my tex' on de tongs ob eberybody in de community from de millionaire down to de licensed vender man. It am written in unmistakable characters and deep lines on de phiz's ob de poor, and in de anxious faces ob de rich. It am none as *Hard Times.*

"*It's hard times,*" tinks de merchant's lady, as she alights from her carriage, decked in a two thousand dollar set ob diamonds, thousand dollar set ob furs, hundred dollar dress, and delicate Opera cloak. It's hard times—husband couldn't afford no greater display, times am so berry hard.

"*It's hard times,*" says the buckish clerk in the Shanghie coat, as he orders oysters and champagne—"Two dozen oysters cooked in warious ways, and only one half-pint bottle ob Hidesick;—times is hard, and I can't afford luxuries."

"*It's hard times,*" says de feller as he pours down Old Hennessy at 25 cents de nip. "De Lord only knows what we am comin' to."

"*It's hard times,*" says de fop to de tailor, "and you must wait." "Hadn't you better wer out your ole close?" says de tailor, "till your finances improve a little, and de times git softer?" "Can't afford it," says de fop, "must hab de Shanghie. I can't afford to lose my position, and look as doe I worked for a libin'."

"*It's hard times,*" says de capitalist, as he buttons up his coat. "I guess I'll lock up what gold and silver I hab in a walt, and luff no man hab it, kase all de

noosepapers says it's hard times and wus a comin'. I'll
lock up my money, kase dere am no noein who to trust.''

''It's hard times,'' says the Bank fellers, who hab bin
libin' too fast, ''and I must eder retrench, or Skiler.
I can't retrench and go in good society arterwards, but I
can default, and in two seasons all am forgotten. I'll
Skiler case it pays best.''

''We must take advantage ob de times,'' says de business man, ''and cut down de wages ob de workman—
now is de time, when noosepapers, preachermen, lawyers,
and eberybody am crying hard times.''

So down goes de wages, and down comes de tears ob
de workman's children for bread at de same time—so
you see de poor man and his family do all de sufferin'
and de rich all de jawin.' Dere am no mistake, de times
am so hard you can bite it.

---

## MY CAROLINA CAROLINE.

Copyright 1901 by Windsor Music Co.  Words and
Music by Billy Johnson.  Music Can be Had of
Windsor Music Co., Chicago.  Price 50c.

—

My gal way down in Carolina, she's all the world to me,
Just like a piece of Dresden china, and my own she soon
    will be,
She's just simply a dusky maiden, lives way down
    'mongst the pine,
My heart with love for her is laden, she's my Caroline.

CHORUS.

My Carolina, Caroline; my angel lady, she's divine;
She's dark complected, highly respected, and she is mine,
    all mine.

If she deceives me, then I'd pine; 'spect 'twould be hard
    to keep me in line;
I'd go distracted, I've been attracted by Carolina
    Caroline.

Me and my gal to-night'll marry; darkies from far and
    near
Have been instructed not to tarry, if they want to see
    and hear,
When we march down the aisle together, everything
    superfine;
On my arm she'll be light as feather my own Caroline.

## GOOD MORNING, CARRIE.

Copyright 1901. Words by R. C. McPherson. Music by
    Smith & Bowen. Order the Music from Windsor
      Music Co., Chicago. Price 50c.

In sunny South Car'lina lives an old Aunt Dinah and
    her daughter named Caroline.
She's winsome, cute and airy; her folks they call her
    Carrie; I hope some day that she'll be mine.
To meet her every evening when the stars are brightly
    beaming, brings joy and pleasure to my heart so
    lone;
In the light of early dawn, with my banjo on my arm, I
    awake her from her slumber with this song:
CHORUS.
Good morning, Carrie; how you do this morning? Was
    you draming 'bout me, pretty maid?
Say, look here, Carrie, when we gwine to marry, long
    spring time, honey,
Good morning, babe.

There's dusky suitors plenty that would take my Carrie
　　from me, out she's promised to be only mine;
With tender songs of wooing, like a turtle dove a-cooing,
　　they serenade my Caroline.
We'll be wedded soon, that's certain, and some hearts
　　will be a-hurtin'
When budding leaves and flowers tell 'tis spring;
There'll be no great display, but on our wedding day,
　　we'll ask the folks around to kindly sing:

---

## I'VE A LONGING IN MY HEART FOR YOU,
## LOUISE.

Copyright 1900.　Arranged by Jos. Clauder.　Words and
　Music by Chas. K. Harris.　Order Your Music from
　　Chas. K. Harris, Milwaukee, Wis.　Price 50c.

---

I've a longing in my heart for you, Louise,
And I wonder if you also think of me,
For your sweet face haunts me ever, dear Louise,
And in dreams I kiss your sweet lips tenderly;
I seem to hear the old church chimes as in the bygone
　　days;
I seem to hear the wihppi'wil's sad lay,
And it brings me back to you, my dear Louise,
And the gentle waving cornfields far away.

### CHORUS.

I've a longing in my heart for you, Louise,
And for the dear old sunny southern home;
I can scent the honeysuckle and the fragrant jessamine;
I've a longing in my heart for you.

Birds are singing 'round the dear old southern home,
And a dark-haired maiden sits beneath a tree,
Thinking of her true love, many miles away,
An she's wondering if he'll ever constant be,
When soft upon the summer breeze she hears her name,
    Louise,
It thrills her heart that beats for him alone.
Then he takes her in his arms so eagerly, and he says:
"I've come to claim you as my own."

## IN THE GOOD OLD-FASHIONED WAY.

Arranged by Jos. Clauder. The Music of This
Song Can be Had from Chas. K. Harris,
Milwaukee, Wis. Price 50c.

In a quaint, old-fashioned homestead, while the snow
    falls fast,
Sits a dear, old loving couple, dreaming of the past.
Tenderly does he caress her, as he used to do,
And he says, "You're still my sweetheart, loving, kind
    and true."
By the fireside they linger, and she heard him say,
"Though we're growing old, I love you more and more
    each day,
Love you in the good fashioned way."

### CHORUS.

For I love you, oh, I love you, in the good fashioned way,
With all a heart's devotion, forever and for aye,
For my love for you grew deeper, when your golden hair
    turned gray,
And I'll love you, always love you, in the good fashioned
    way.

And how well do I remember days of long ago,
To the little village school-house you and I would go;
I can see the roses blooming, round your home and mine,
And the fragrant fields of clover in that southern clime.
Fifty years have passed, my darling, since that night in
    May,
When I told you that I loved you, as I do to-day;
Love you, in the good old-fashioned way.

---

## THE MANSION OF ACHING HEARTS.

Copyright 1902. Words by Arthur J. Lamb. Sheet
Music 50c. Order from Harry Von Tilgen Music
Pub. Co., 42 W. 28th St., New York.

---

The last dance was over, the music had ceased, and the
    dancers were leaving the hall;
A few men were saying their last goodbyes to the beau-
    tiful belle of the ball;
Alone by the window a youth sadly stands, his heart she
    had stolen away,
And just as he gazed on her beautiful face,
He was startled to hear some one say:

CHORUS.

She lives in a mansion of aching hearts; she's one of the
    restless throng;
The diamonds that glitter around her throat, they speak
    of both sorrow and song—
The smile on her face is only a mask, and many a tear
    that starts,
For sadder it seems, when of mother she dreams
In the mansion of aching hearts.

Alone by a fireside a man sadly looks at a picture that
hangs on the wall;
He has never forgotten the sad, sweet face of the beau-
tiful belle of the ball;
He's reading her letter, "My picture I send; I have
loved you, but only in vain;
Oh, try to forget that we ever have met,"
Then he thinks with a heart full of pain:

---

## WAKE UP, MA BABY.

### SONG AND CAKEWALK.

Copyright, 1899, by Ascher, Schott & Bowsky. Royal
Music Co. Words by Harvey A. Wood. Music by
Emil Archer. English Copyright Secured.

---

Ma baby's de best cake-walker you'll find,
Her style is just de real swell kind,
But only one thing bothers ma mind,
    She drives me crazy, she's so lazy.
Right in a cake walk she starts to creep,
Sometimes I think she's fast asleep,
Den fur to rouse her I have to keep
    Shoutin' wid all ma might: "O!"

### CHORUS.

Wake up, ma baby, wake up, ma gal,
Wake up, ma honey, step lively, Sal;
I made a bet dat you'd get the cake,
You'll do it too, babe, if you keep wide awake."

When I tell her once I never repeat,
Then, when she starts to move her feet,
All hands agree dat she can't be beat;

Now make no blunder; she's a wonder;
Most every coon dat watches us knows
How much ma baby likes to dose,
An' so she'll get no chance to repose,
They start de same old shout: "O!"—CHORUS.

---

## JUST BECAUSE SHE MADE THEM GOO-GOO EYES.

Parody—Written and Sung by Harry S. Sargent.

A rube dressed in his Sunday clothes regardless of ex-
pense,
Blew into a poker joint, because he hadn't any sense;
But lit out quick, down on his luck.
A damsel flagged him on the run, and said, "come play
with me;"
He says, "though I've been buncoed, still, by gosh, your
hand I'll see,
What have you got? ge whiz, I'm stuck."

### CHORUS.

Just because she made dem goo-goo eyes, she did up
quick a chap about my size;
Now I wish I had that roll, and the watch and chain she
stole,
Just because she made dem goo-goo eyes.

My uncle died in Europe, and left me all his cash,
But how to get it over here, so I could cut a dash,
Has troubled me, drove me to drink.
I went to see a lawyer, and I stated him my case,
He said, "My boy, you're bug house, you're completely
off your base;
Just think it over, but I don't think."

CHORUS.

Just because I made dem goo-goo eyes, that lawyer chap
  thought I was telling lies;
But never mind, I guess, I'll think it over by express,
  Just because I made dem goo-goo eyes.

---

## WHEN THE HARVEST DAYS ARE OVER.

Parody—Written and Sung by Harry S. Sargent.

—

There's a young man sad and tearful, though he once
  was bright and cheerful,
  When he thought he'd sit March fourth in Washington;
But free silver downed poor Billy, and McKinley
  knocked him silly,
  While Mark Hanna and the trusts they grabbed the
  bun.
When the harvest days are over, you can bet they'll be
  in clover,
  For they'll reap for four years more both night and
  day;
When the crop is cut they'll shake it, while the voters
  grin and bear it,
  And when the jig is up you'll hear them say:

CHORUS.

Now the harvest days are over, Hanna, dear,
  Off to Europe on a pleasure trip we'll steer,
With our wealth we'll play the deuce, for Uncle Sam
  we've got no use,
  Now the harvest days are over, Hanna, dear.

There's an old man sad and weary, sick and tired of life
    so dreary,
  He is dreaming of the wealth he never had;
He has raised up fourteen children, but now wishes he
    had killed 'em,
  For the blooming kids have all gone to the bad.
'Tis the sad and oft-told story, of the children in their
    glory,
  While the parents, who have raised them up, go broke,
And the mother softly sighing, dropped her false teeth
    in her crying,
  While the old man grabbed her by the hair and spoke:

CHORUS.
Now the harvest days are over, Jessie, dear.
  To the poor house we will rusticate, so near;
But let me tell you here, for once, we'll never raise an-
    other bunch,
For our harvest days are over, Jessie, dear.

---

## DAT BAD MAN BROWN.

Words and Music by Maude Evelyn Moulton.
—

In de town whar I belongs, dere lives a man named
    Brown,
Talk about de wild man, he could throw de hull crowd
    down;
Air turns blue when he gets mad, the cops, you bet, dey
    sneak;

Dere's none around, dey can't be found, when dey hear
   dat coon speak.

CHORUS.

For dere's no coon in town can get de best of Brown,
He's de wildest coon dat eber walked, de meanest man
   dat eber talked;
De dogs an' children fly, an' old maids almost die;
When he appears dey're all in tears, dat bad man Brown.

Brown once loved a yaller gal, she didn't dare say no,
Begged de parson on de sly to save her from de foe;
Dey came for de weddin', parson 'fused to do de act;
Now parson's whar de good folks go, he'll nebber more
   come back.—CHORUS.

---

### HELLO, MY BABY.

Parody by Martin J. Kane.

I'se got a little clothing store, but it's on the bum,
   Although I've got it heavily insured,
The policy must be renewed or out it will run,
   I'm getting crazy, it cannot be endured;
This morning everybody heard me yell
   This afternoon this policy does expire;
My heart goes blankety blank when I hear a bell,
   Because I think it is a fire.

CHORUS.

Hello, my Abe, I need some money; hello, my insurance
   pal;
Send me a policy by wire, my home will soon be a-fire;
If you refuse me, Rebecca will lose me, then she'll be all
   alone;
   O, Abe, send it, and I can burn my home.

He never was at a telephone in his life before,
   And mixed things up, as you can judge,
The policy they sent him was 4-11-44—
   From the 'phone he would not budge;
He shook all over like an aspen leaf,
   And a salty tear came to his eye,
But he soon was full of joy instead of grief
   When he heard somebody cry:

CHORUS.

Hello, my Isaac, du bist sehr fleisig, wie ist dein
      gescheft?
   I send you some policy by wire—it's a winner or I'm
      a liar;
If you don't do it, den you will rue it, so you will then
      get left;
   O, Isaac, play it, und you don't need one fire.

---

## LET ME GO BACK CHILLUN.

Copyright, 1899, by Hamilton S. Gordon.   English Copy-
right Secured.   Used by Permission of Hamilton S.
Gordon, 189 Fifth Ave., N. Y.   Price 50 cents.
Words and Music by Minnie F. Howard.

Yes, I 'spec's I'se old an' childish now, when de win'
      blows down de leaves,
   An' de wild birds plume dere pinions fer ter fly;
Oh, it's den dis po' ol' darkey's heart wid de homesick
      longin' grieves,
   An' I wants ter see de ol' home 'fore I die.

REFRAIN.

Let me go back chillun to dat sunny southern 'lan',
De wild birds am flown dar long ago,
An' de ol' friends am waiting in dat cottage on de hill,
Whar de red roses bloom above de do'.

Oh, de frost am on de window pane, oh, de cold ma heart
am chillin',
An' de garden am all kivered white wid snow;
But down dar de birds am singin' sweet, an' de flowers
bloom, yo' know,
In de lan' down whar de orange blossoms grow.

REFRAIN.

---

## LITTLE YALLER LOU.

Copyright, 1899, by Hamilton S. Gordon. English Copyright Secured. Used by Permission of Hamilton S.
Gordon, 139 Fifth Ave., N. Y. Price 50 cents.
Words and Music by Maude Evelyn Moulton.

---

I fell right dead in love wid de sweetest little dove,
Little Lulu Snow from Tennessee;
She made a slave of me, an' from her I'se never free,
I'd do anything she'd ask me to.
De money I did save, to dat yaller gal I gave,
For to keep till we was wed;
She tole me dat nobody'd get away dat cash,
"I'll take good care of dat," she said.

CHORUS.

She's de cutest gal in all dis world I know,
If you met her you would say dat it was so,
Oh, Lulu, Lulu, ev'ry day I pines for you, no other gal
will do,
All I'se got is yours for life, my litle yaller Lou.

A week ago dat Lou wid anudder nigger flew,
    Took ma money too, all dat I had;
She broke ma heart in two, when I heard dat she had
    flew.
    Do you wonder dat I feel so bad?
She told me not to cry, 'kase she didn't say good-bye,
    But she'd take care of dat red;
An' nobody would get de cash away from her,
    She'd keep her word to me she said.—CHORUS.

------

## MY DARKTOWN BELLE.

Copyright, 1900, by Wulschner Music Co.
By Fred Mower and Roy Burtch.

------

I'm in love with Susie Sweetbird, she's the dearest girl
    in town,
        How I love my darktown belle;
She's the queen of all de cakewalks, her complexion's
    chestnut brown,
        How I love my darktown belle;
She's de belle of all the parties, sings or cuts de pigeon
    wing,
Now all the boys am crazy, for to buy a wedding ring,
        They all love ma darktown belle.

### CHORUS.

She's my only true love, dat cause my heart to swell,
Love has no color, either black, white or yeller, and I
    love ma darktown belle.

When with Susie I am talking, in my throat dar comes a
    lump,

How I love my darktown belle;
When at me she smiles so sweetly, den my heart goes
bump, bump,
How I love my darktown belle;
When I asked her if she'd be mine, she looked right
into my eyes,
Said "Yes, I'm yours my honey"—den I knew I'd won
my prize,
How I love ma darktown belle.

----

## I'D LEAVE MY HAPPY HOME FOR YOU.
### Parody by Chris Lane.

Last night I went into a restaurant,
I was feeling rather hungry I'll admit,
The pork chops were on the hog, I was hungry as a dog,
So anything to eat would make a hit.
To my stomach I did cater so I ordered from a waiter,
An oyster stew with crackers on the side
Said I, this is a treat, but when I began to eat,
An oyster cracker from the bowl replied:

### CHORUS.
I leave my happy home for you-oo-oo-oo-oo,
That cracker was a cracker jack that's true-oo-oo-oo-oo,
It said take me and just break me in that oyster stew-oo,
I'd leave this cracker bowl for you-oo-oo-oo-oo.

A big tom cat in a yard sat,
The hour it was very near midnight,
He warbled a song the whole night long,
Till the neighbors they were mad enough to fight,
A brickbat from above could not keep him from love,

Or a water pitcher that had missed his head,
He sang, meow, meow, I'm waiting here for you,
In a feline tenor voice Maria said:

CHORUS.

I leave my happy home for you, me-ew, me-ew,
You're the sweetest Tom I ever knew, me-ew, me-ew.
Tom drew nigher to Maria, and sang, I love you too,
    mew,
I'd leave my happy home for you, me-ew, me-ew.

---

## RAG-TIME RASTUS, THE WHISTLER.
Words and Music by Lester S. Parker.
Copyright 1900.
All rights reserved.

Oh Rastus Johnson called his dog,
Went out for to find a coon:
Dinah hollered at Rastus, you nigga; you come home
    soon!
    He answered to her mandate, by whistling to the
        moon,
    By whistling loud and cheerfully, his old familiar tune.

He wandered thro' the timber, he sauntered thro' the
    cane,
No thought of care or worry, e'er crossed that nigger's
    brain,
His hungry stomach urged him, to hustle for a coon,
But the only thought he gave it, was the whistling of
    this tune.

When weary of his walking, he laid his body down,
And soon was sleeping soundly, stretched out upon the
    ground,
But when he woke next morning, the sun was high at
    noon,
Though scared at Dinah's welcome home, he whistled out
    this tune.

When Dinah got the nigger home, she cracked him on the
    head;
She combed his hair with the garden rake, she kicked him
    under the bed,
She danced a cake walk on his back, she pitched him
    from the room,
And when he struck the ground outside, he whistled out
    this tune.

---

## ALL I WANTS IS MY BLACK BABY BACK.

Copyright, 1898, by Howley, Haviland & Co. English
Copyright secured.
By Gus Edwards and Tom Daly.

---

A dark-town belle and her yeller man had a terr'ble fuss,
Because she called this big black coon a lazy cuss,
He got right mad and left the house without a word to
    say,
And she's been hunting 'round the town for him 'most
    every day,
He says he's done with her and won't come back no more,
He's goin' back to his other gal in Baltimore,
The wench is crazy and pining for him most ev'ry day,
And ev'ry one she meets these words she'll say—

CHORUS.

All I wants is my black baby back,
He's the sweetest man and that's a fact,
You can have all of my money,
If you'll only find my honey,
All I wants is my black baby back.

She said she didn't think her man would run away,
Because she didn't mean a word that she did say,
She was only foolin' when she hit him with a brick,
And for her big black man this baby's getting awful
  sick,
And now her room rent's due and she ain't got a cent,
For he took ev'ry dollar of hers before he went
If he will only come back she will never do wrong,
And never have to sing again this song.—*Chorus.*

---

## I'SE GETTIN' UP A WATERMELON PARTY.

Copyright, 1899, by Hamilton S. Gordon.  English Copyright secured.

Used by Permission of Hamilton S. Gordon, 139 Fifth
Ave., N. Y.  Price 50 cents.

Words and Music by Keller Brothers

---

I'se a-gettin' up a watermelon party,
    For I'se gwine to celebrate my honeymoon;
Ev'ry ev'nin' I'se a-givin' my instructions,
    All de neighborhood is talkin' 'bout dis coon.
I'se proud 'cause I'se full of 'riginality,
    An' particula' in ev'rything I do;
Dar'll be colored invitations for all my relations.
    An' a gilt-edge one for you.

CHORUS.

When you get your invitation to my melon party,
Bring along your lady love, a-feelin' well an' hearty.
Dar's a gwine to be a cake walk, dancin' music, oh, so
fine,
On a moonlight eve we's all a gwine to leave, an' carve
dem melons on de vine.

I'se a-gettin' up a watermelon party,
An' I'se gwine to seat you all in parlor chairs;
My professor's gone into de proper trainin',
An' his colored band will play de latest airs.
My gal she's a gwine to wear her weddin' gown,
An' together we will do a fancy turn;
So when I bring in Dinah, de music will be finer,
An' de lights will brighter burn.—CHORUS.

## SONGS FOR SINGERS.

### MY OLD KENTUCKY MOME.

The sun shines bright in the old Kentucky home,
'Tis Summer, the darkies are gay;
The corn top's ripe and the meadow's in the bloom,
While the birds make music all the day.
The young folks roll on the little cabin floor,
All merry, all happy and bright;
By'n by hard times comes a-knocking at the door,
Then, my old Kentucky home, good-night.

CHORUS.

Weep no more, my lady, oh! weep no more to-day!
We will sing one song for the old Kentucky home,
For the old Kentucky home, far away.

They hunt no more for the possum and the coon
  On the meadow, the hill and the shore;
They sing no more, by the glimmer of the moon,
  On the beach by the old cabin-door.
The day goes by, like a shadow o'er the heart,
  With sorrow where all was delight;
The time has come when the darkies have to part;
  Then, my old Kentucky home, good-night.

The head must bow and the back will bend,
  Wherever the darkey may go;
A few more days, and the trouble all will end
  In the field where the sugar canes grow;
A few more days for to tote the weary load,
  No matter, 'twill never be light,
A few more days we'll totter on the road;
  Then, my old Kentucky home, good-night.

---

## SLEEP MY LITTLE 'SIMMIN COLORED COON.

Written and composed by William H. Plass.
—

Chickens am a-roostin' in de old plum tree,
  One by one de little stars am peeping;
  Nightingales am singin' to my babe and me,
Brightly shines de silver moon.
  Time my little pickaniny am at rest,
  All de little birds am sleeping;
  Mammy's gwine to tuck you in your little feather nest,
Den she's gwine to softly croon.
  Slumber, little nigger, in your bed so cozy,

Mammy's gwine to wake you when de moon am rosy.
Hush, my little baby love, sleep, my rosebud,
Angels guard you from above, sleep, my little nut-brown
    coon.

### CHORUS.

Sleep, sleep, sleep, my little yaller baby, mammy loves
    you so,
Close your naughty little eyelids, you'se de sweetest little
    coon I know;
Great, big 'gaiters gwine to eat you if you don't hush
    mighty soon,
'Deen dey knows it when my baby cries, sleep, my little
    'simmon colored coon.

Juicy ripe persimmon's mighty fine to eat,
    Waiting for my baby in de morning;
Just about de color of my baby, so sweet,
Honey gwine to eat dem soon.
    'Gaiters am uneasy when dey hears you weep,
    Mind, I gives you timely warning;
    Mammy's gwine to rock her little dusky babe to sleep,
While she sings de sandman's tune.
    'Deed I loves my bandy-legged, sweet, brown baby,
    Even tho' his color am a trifle shady.
    Hush, my little turtle dove, sleep, my rosebud;
Angels guard you from above, sleep, my little nut-brown
    coon.

---

### OLD OAKEN BUCKET.

#### FOR QUARTET.

How dear to this heart are the scenes of my childhood,
    When fond recollections recall them to view;
The orchard, the meadow, the deep-tangled wildwood,

Every loved spot which my infancy knew;
The wide spreading pond, and the mill which stood by it
  The bridge, and the rock where the cataract fell,
The cot of my father, the dairy-house nigh it,
  And e'en the rude bucket which hung in the well.
The old oaken bucket—the iron-bound bucket—
  The moss-covered bucket, which hung in the well.

The moss-covered vessel I hailed as a treasure,
  For often, at noon, when returned from the field,
I found it the source of an exquisite pleasure,
  The purest and sweetest that nature can yield;
How ardent I seized it, with hands that were glowing,
  And quick to the white-pebbled bottom it fell,
Then soon, with the emblem of truth overflowing,
  And dripping with coolness, it rose from the well.
The old oaken bucket—the iron-bound bucket—
  The moss-covered bucket arose from the well.

How sweet from the green mossy brim to receive it,
  As poised on the curb, it inclined to my lips;
Not a full-blushing goblet could tempt me to leave it,
  Though filled with the nectar that Jupiter sips.
And now far removed from the loved situation,
  The tear of regret will intrusively swell,
As fancy revisits my father's plantation,
  And sighs for the bucket which hangs in the well.
The old oaken bucket—the iron-bound bucket—
  The moss-covered bucket which hangs in the well.

## SHORT VERSE FOR END-MEN.

### HIS LAST CIGAR.

A small boy puffed at a big cigar,
  His eyes bulged out and his cheeks sank in,
He gulped rank fumes with his lips ajar,
  While muscles shook in his youthful chin;
His gills were green but he smole a smile,
And sat right up on the farmyard style,
And cocked his hat o'er his glassy eye,
Then wunk a wink at a sow near by.

The earth swam round, but the stye stood still;
  The trees rose up and the kid slid down;
He groaned aloud, for he felt so ill,
  And he knew that cigar had "done him brown;"
His head was light and his feet like lead,
His cheeks grew white as a linen spread,
  While he weakly gasped, as he gazed afar,
"If I live, this here's my last cigar."

### THE MELLOW MELLON.

A green watermelon sat on a fruit stand,
  Singing "Mellow, I'm mellow, I'm mellow;"
And a small boy stood there with a cent in his hand,
  Saying "Mellow, its mellow, quite mellow."
So he ate a big hunk cut right out of the heart,
And he ate it all up to the hard outside part,
And they carried him off in a rag-dealer's cart,
  Poor fellow, poor fellow, poor fellow.

### THE LOST DOG.

A lady lost her dog last week,
  And this week when she went
To interview the butcher on
  The style of meat for Lent,

He pointed to a sausage link—
The lady turned to look,
And when she said she'd take it home,
It wagged right off the hook.

### THE CIGARETTE.

I am only a small cigarette,
But my work I will get in, you bet,
    For the stern coffin maker
    And grim undertaker
Will declare I bring fish to their net.

### ODD SEE-SAWS.

I saw a cow-hide in the grass,
    A rush-light in the floor;
I saw a candle-stick in mud,
    And a bell-pull on the door.

I saw a horse-fly up the creek,
    A cat-nip at her food;
I saw a chestnut-burr, and heard
    A shell-bark in the wood.

I saw a jack-plane off a board
    A car-spring off the track;
I saw a saw-dust off the floor,
    And then a carpet-tack.

I saw a monkey-wrench a hat
    From a fair lady's pate;
I saw a rattle-snake a bird,
    And hogs-head on a plate.

I saw a brandy-smash a glass,
    I saw a shooting-star;
I heard the corns-talk in the field,
    A pig-iron crow bar.

### HER ALL TOO SOLID LOVE.

A St. Louis maid threw her lover a kiss,
A St. Louis kiss which they brag on,
It hit the young man on the side of the head
And knocked him cold off the wagon.
The coroner said it was hardly worth while
To proceed to impanel a jury,
Since no man could stand being hit by a kiss
The size of the map of Missouri.

### HE AIN'T BUILT THAT WAY.

Some girls can look upon a mouse
And neither scream nor faint,
They can, there's no denying;
But where's the man can pass a house
Which bears the warning "Paint,"
Without a test applying?

### OLD SAWS IN RHYME.

Actions speak louder than words ever do;
You can't eat your cake and hold on to it, too.

When the cat is away then the little mice play;
When there is a will there is always a way.

One's deep in the mud as the other in mire;
Don't jump from the frying pan into the fire.

There's no use crying over milk that is spilt;
No accuser is needed by conscience of guilt.

There must be some fire wherever is smoke;
The pitcher goes oft to the well till it's broke.

By rogues falling out honest men get their dues;
Whoever it fits he must put on the shoe.

All work and no play will make Jack a dull boy;
A thing of much beauty is ever a joy.

A half loaf is better than no bread at all;
And pride always goeth before a sad fall.

### A CHRISTMAS DINNER.

Unto a little nigger,
    A-swimming in the Nile,
Appeared, quite unexpectedly,
    A hungry crocodile,
Who, with that chilled politeness
    That makes the warm blood freeze,
Remarked, "I'll take some dark meat
    Without dressing, if you please!"

### A STRAY EPITAPH.

Here does the body of Mary. Anne rest,
With her head on Abraham's breast,
It's a very good thing for Mary Anne,
But it's very hard lines for Abraham.

The boy stood on the back yard fence,
Whence all but him had fled.
The fire that burned his father's barn,
Shone brightly o'er his head.
A bunch of fire-crackers in his hand,
And two others in his hat.
He cried out in accent wild
I never thought of that.
A bunch of fire-crackers to a small dog he tied,
The dog in anger sought the barn,
And there amongst the ruins died.
The flames grew fierce and hot,

As they lit on the brat,
And set the crackers off in his hand,
And likewise those in his hat.
Hark! A rattling sound is heard,
But the boy, oh, where was he?
Ask of the winds that scatter the fragments o'er the sea.
'Midst scraps of cloth and balls and dots,
And nails and yarn,
Was the eventful fate of that dreadful boy
Who burned his father's barn.

A potato went out on a mash,
    And sought out an onion bed;
"That's pie for me," observed the squash,
    And all the beets turned red.
"Go away," the onion weeping cried,
    "Your love I cannot be;
The pumpkin is your lawful bride,
    You cantalope (can't elope) with me."

---

## THE WAY DIFFERENT GIRLS KISS.

The New York girl bows her stately head,
    And fixes her stylish lips
In a firm, hard way—and lets 'em go,
    And sips, and sips, and sips.

The Baltimore girl has a way of her own,
    In a clinging, soulful way,
She takes a kiss that just as big,
    As a wagon load of hay.

The Chicago girl gets a grip on herself
    And carefully takes off her hat,

Then grabs the man in a frenzied way,
Like a terrier shaking a rat.

The Boston girl takes off her specs,
So cool—so cold—so glum.
She sticks out her lips—like an open book,
And keeps on chewing gum.

The Philadelphia girl never says a word,
She's so gentle—timid and tame.
But she grabs a young man by the back of the neck,
And gets there, just the same.

## CAKE WALKS.

Cake walks have become such a popular craze during the last few years that society everywhere are introducing them in their many social events, and minstrel performances now seem incomplete without them. While it is a difficult matter to explain everything connected with the many movements, etc., in a cake walk, the author has used his best endeavors to make it plain to the reader. In the first place, to successfully take part in a cake walk, each participant should take great pains in your make-up. The most extreme and flashy suits should be worn, including an endless variety of diamonds or Rhine stones, for jewelry effects. The young lady or young man that takes such part should wear bright colored dresses. Large hat and high heel slippers and carry parasol or fan which will show off in excellent taste. The gentleman partner should wear a Prince Albert coat made of red, blue, brown or green satin, high silk hat of same material, checked trousers, patent leather shoes with white gaiters, a cane with crooked handle, decorated with ribbons of same colors as his lady's dress. Where more than one couple take part, try and have your costumes, both ladies and gentlemen, different from one another.

## THE WALK.

Start your walk by taking partner's hand, elevating it to about the height of your head; step off somewhat in advance of lady, assuming a happy smile; keep step with each time of the music, and be sure to step only on ball of foot, letting the heel down gently as you touch the other foot to the floor. After passing the audience once in that position let go of hands and continue to walk alone, meeting again at front of audience with bow. Lady will then take your arm and continue walk halfway round when she discovers her shoe untied. You will then proceed with much grace and a bow. Kneeling, place your handkerchief upon your knee, and placing lady's foot thereon, proceed to tie it, after which he will arise and accept a kiss which she will offer. The most essential point in a cake walk is to always keep your face towards the audience, no matter if walking directly away from them with your backs turned.

Put in your walks as many different steps or figures as possible, such as imitating an old colored man, a Hebrew, a German, etc., and always bear in mind that the hands, arms and face have as much to do with your success as the walking part. A graceful swing of the arms, or if carried out away from the body, is always clever. Where you have four couples and wish to end the walk as an entertaining finish, use the cake walk quadrille following:

---

## CAKE WALK QUADRILLE.

### (The Popular Fad of Popular Society.)

Figures by Prof. A. C. Wirth, President of the American National Association of Masters of Dancing. Music composed and arranged by Wm. Wirth. Copyrighted 1899.

### FIRST FIGURE.

Address partners and center (a la Cake Walk) [8 measures]; first four right and left with right hand couple [8]; promenade with same (Cake Walk) [8]; ladies chain [8]; four ladies cross right hands and circle around the inside of the set. (Simultaneously the four gents promenade single file around the set in opposite direction.) Call it thus: Ladies cross right hands, circle. Gents promenade outside. Cake Walk [8]; side four repeat with the right hand couple.

### SECOND FIGURE.

Commence figure with second strain of music. First couple cake walk inside of set [8 measures]; all march single file to the right around the set [8]; third couple cake walk inside of set [8]; all march single file to left around the set [8]; second and fourth couples the same.

### THIRD FIGURE.

Commence figures with second strain of music. First couple promenade inside of set, cake walk, face out, third and fourth couple fall in line [8]; separate in two lines, head couple cake walk down the center and back [8]; forward and back, in two lines [4]; turn partners to place [4]; all promenade (cake walk) around the set [8]. Four times. The third, second and fourth couples promenade inside of set and face out in the order named.

### FOURTH FIGURE.

Commence figures with music. Join hands, circle to the left [8 measures]; first couple promenade around the outside of set, a la cake walk [8]; first couple inside of set, six hands around [8]; four ladies cross right hands in center, left hand to gent's right, promenade around in a star (cake walk) [8]; third couple promenade around, outside, cake walk [8]; third couple inside of set, six hands around [8]; four gents cross right hands in center, left hand to lady's right, all promenade in star, cake walk [8].

No. 4, except circle to the left, is repeated by the second and fourth couples, in the place of first and third. To finish, all forward and back. Address center, a la cake walk. All two-step around the hall.

### THE END.

# Frederick J. Drake & Company's

## CATALOGUE OF

# Standard Up=to=Date Hand Books
# on the following Subjects:

**Dialogues, Recitations, Tableaux,
Charades, Pantomimes, Mock Trials,
Monologues, Drills, Marches, Minstrel
and Entertainment Books, Magic,
Palmistry, Hypnotism, Black Art,
Electricity, Speakers, Poultry,
Letter Writers, Dream Books,
Fortune Tellers, Popular Dramas,
Photography, Etiquette, Dancing,
Etc., Etc., Etc., Etc.**

---

Each book in this list is the work of a competent specialist, and will be found reliable, practical and thoroughly up-to-date.

---

**Any Book Advertised in This Catalogue Sent,
Postpaid, on Receipt of Price.
FREDERICK J. DRAKE & CO.,
211-213 EAST MADISON ST., Chicago.
SEND FOR COMPLETE CATALOGUE.**

# Frederick J. Drake & Co.

## New Century Series of Popular Up-to-Date Books . . . . . .

You can derive more solid, practical and valuable instruction from this series of little books than from any other source.

Each book is printed from new, large type, on a fine quality of wove paper, making them the very best yet offered to our customers.

## BROWN'S BUSINESS LETTER WRITER AND BOOK OF SOCIAL FORMS.

By C. W. Brown, A. M. The most complete practical compendium of correspondence and business forms ever published. Gives full instructions for writing, and specimens of Business Letters, Legal Forms, Leases, Deeds, Wills, Contracts; models for Refined Love-Letters, covering Courtship, Engagements, Marriage; Social Forms, Invitations, Acceptances, Regrets, Condolences; Family Letters for Parents, Guardians and Children; How to address the President and Government Officials. Also leading synonyms. It will tell you anything you really need in the way of a letter. 208 pages.

Paper Covers.................................25 Cents
Cloth, Gold Titles...........................50 Cents

## NORTH'S BOOK OF LOVE LETTERS.

With directions how to write and when to use them. By Ingoldsby North. This is a branch of correspondence which fully demands a volume alone to provide for the various phases incident to Love, Courtship and Marriage. Few persons, however otherwise fluent with the pen, are able to express in words the promptings of the first dawn of love, and even, the ice broken, how to follow up a correspondence with the dearest one in the whole world and how to smooth the way with those who need to be consulted in the matter. It also contains the Art of Secret Writing. The language of Love portrayed, and rules in grammar. 160 pages.

Paper Covers...................................25 Cents
Cloth...........................................50 Cents

## PRACTICAL ETIQUETTE.

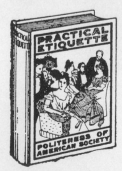

A strictly modern book on politeness. Just what one needs to keep in touch with what is "Correct" at the present time. Hints on politeness and good breeding, sensible talks about etiquette for home, visiting, sensible talks about parties, evening entertainments, social intercourse, dress, etc. No part in daily conduct has been omitted. The immense popularity of this little book is attested by its enormous sales. It is an invaluable adjunct to any home and will be found exceedingly helpful in the hands of parents and teachers as well as young people of both sexes. 160 pages.

Paper Covers....................................25 Cents
Cloth, Gold Titles..............................50 Cents

### IRISH WIT AND HUMOR.
Irish wit and humor is a factor in human experience which the world can ill afford to lose. In some of its qualities it is second to the wit and humor of no nation on earth. Judging it by its average specimens—and it would be manifestly misleading to take a lower standard—it manages to convey an idea fully; but in its haste to express itself,—the mataphors get mixed, and the thoughts transposed or reversed. For playfulness, for sarcastic keenness, for gracefulness, and for red-hot scornfulness, nothing is more effective than some of the examples of the wit and humor of the Irishman, as told in this timely volume. Amateur theatricals or entertainments of any character will find this book a most acceptable addition for gathering material. 160 pages.

Paper Covers..........................................25 Cents
Cloth, Gold Titles....................................50 Cents

### CONUNDRUMS AND RIDDLES.

Collected and arranged by John Ray. This is the latest, largest and best collection of Conundrums ever published. Containing upwards of four thousand choice new intellectual Conundrums and Riddles which will sharpen your wit and lead you to think quickly. They are always a source of great amusement and pleasure, whiling away tedious hours and putting every one in a general good humor. Any person, with the assistance of this book, may take the lead in entertaining a company and keep them in roars of laughter for hours. We heartily recommend it to amateurs and professionals for entertainments of all kinds. 160 pages.

Paper Covers..........................................25 Cents
Cloth, Gilt Titles....................................50 Cents

### NEGRO MINSTRELS.
By Jack Haverly. A complete handbook written to encourage, help and guide amateurs in their efforts to form troupes and give a successful evening's performance. An entire program is arranged with full details, consisting of a first part with the brightest dialogue between "Tambo," "Bones" and the "Middleman"; the introduction of ballads, songs, gags, conundrums, side-splitting stump speeches, etc. Mr. Jack Haverly was one of the most widely experienced men on the minstrel stage, and in this book has drawn on his stock of tried features, selecting and offering his best therefrom. 150 pages.

Paper Covers ...............................25 Cents
Cloth, Gilt Titles ...........................50 Cents

Any book in this list sent postpaid to any address upon receipt of price
Complete Catalogue sent free.

## FREDERICK J. DRAKE & CO., Publishers
### 211-213 EAST MADISON ST., CHICAGO

## PHOTOGRAPHY SELF-TAUGHT.

By T. Stith Baldwin. The camera is now recognized as a factor in the fields of pleasure, profit and instruction and is used by every class of citizen; by the tourist and other pleasure seekers as an adjunct to further the enjoyment of a vacation and to provide lasting souvenirs of a pleasant experience.

Any man, woman or child of ordinary intelligence, without previous experience, by simply following printed instructions, can soon acquire the knowledge necessary to properly operate the camera, develop the plate (or film), and print and finish the picture. 160 pages, 59 illustrations.

Paper Covers............................ ......25 Cents
Cloth.........................................50 Cents

## STANDARD PERFECTION POULTRY BOOK

By C. C. Shoemaker. The recognized standard work on poultry in this country, containing a complete description of all the varieties of fowls, including turkeys, ducks, and geese with illustrations of each; poultry houses and how to build them, also full directions for operating incubators and brooders.

Chapters on diseases, feeding, caponizing, dressing and shipping and fattening for market. Sites for buildings, land needed, etc., etc. 200 pages, 80 illustrations.

Paper Covers................................ ..25 Cents
Cloth.........................................50 Cents

## COMPLETE DEBATERS' MANUAL.

By Charles Walter Brown, A. M. This book will fill a place occupied by no other. It is not only a manual of parliamentary usages but a complete guide to all matters pertaining to Organization. Debating Clubs will find this book unequaled. It tells us all about how to start the machinery. How to outline and prepare a debate. It gives full debates, so that the inexperienced speaker may know about what he is expected to say, and how much is required to fill his allotted time. 160 pages.

Paper Covers ...............................25 Cents
Cloth, Gilt Titles...........................50 Cents

Any book in this list sent postpaid to any address upon receipt of price.
Complete Catalogue sent free.

# FREDERICK J. DRAKE & CO., Publishers
## 211-213 EAST MADISON ST., CHICAGO

## LITTLE FOLKS' DIALOGUES & DRAMAS.

By Charles Walter Brown, A. M. A collection of original Dialogues and Dramas by various authors, sprightly and sensible, particularly adapted for little people from three to twelve years old, on subjects and ideas fitted to their age, handled in the quaint manner and appropriate action so often observed in even children of tender age. Suitable for all occasions. Special day celebrations, etc. With costumes for boys and girls. 180 pages.

Paper Covers..................................25 Cents
Cloth, Gold Titles ...........................50 Cents

## CHOICE DIALECT AND VAUDEVILLE STAGE JOKES.

Containing side-splitting Stories, Readings, Recitations, Jokes, Gags and Monologues, in Irish, Dutch, Scotch, Yankee, French, Italian, Spanish, Negro, and other dialects, representing every phase of sentiment from the keenest humor or the tenderest pathos to that which is strongly dramatic. We heartily recommend this book to amateurs and professionals as being the Best, Latest and containing the brightest dialect stories of the vaudeville stage, as told and recited by Ezra Kendall, George Thatcher, Lew Dockstader, Rogers Bros., Weber and Fields, Joe Welsh and others. 200 pages.

Paper Covers...........................................25 Cents
Cloth, Gold Titles .....................................50 Cents

## DUTCH DIALECT.

Recitations, Readings and Jokes, as told by our foremost vaudeville stars, Weber and Fields, Rogers Brothers, Marshall P. Wilder, Ezra Kendall, Geo. Fuller Golden, Gus Williams and others. Every lover of German dialect, wit and humor ought to procure a copy of this new and up-to-date book, as it contains the choicest emanations of the most celebrated and renowned Dutch comedians and humorists of the present day. Rip-roaring, side-splitting Dutch dialect. Hot humor covers its many pages, and comedians and amateurs who wish to keep an audience or social gathering in a continuous stream of laughter and merriment, and receive tumultuous applause at every appearance, will find in this book exactly what they require. 130 pages.

Paper Covers.................. ..................................25 Cents
Cloth, Gold Titles................. ........................50 Cents

Any book in this list sent postpaid to any address upon receipt of price. Complete Catalogue sent free.

# FREDERICK J. DRAKE & CO., Publishers
## 211-213 EAST MADISON ST., CHICAGO

## STANDARD DRILL & MARCHING BOOK.

By Edwin Ellis. Containing an endless variety of new, original drills and marches for young people. Each being illustrated with diagrams easy to understand. No form of entertainment has proved itself more Amusing, Healthful or Popular than "Standard Drills and Marches." The author has included all of the very latest and most amusing drills and marches known. 160 pages, 30 illustrations.

Illustrated Paper Covers........................25 Cents
Cloth Covers, Gold Titles.......................50 Cents

## ZANCIG'S NEW COMPLETE PALMISTRY.

The only authorized edition published. By Prof. and Mme. Zancig. Here we have the simplest presentations of the Science of Modern Palmistry. All of the discoveries, investigations and researches of centuries are summed up in this practical treatise on Palmistry. There is no trait, no characteristic, no inherited tendency that is not marked on the palm of the hand, and can be traced with unerring accuracy by following the principles and instructions laid down in this book. 200 pages; 86 fine illustrations. N. B.—Other editions bearing the name of Zancigs are not authorized by them.

Paper Covers................................25 Cents
Cloth, Titles in Gold.........................50 Cents

## THE GYPSY WITCH DREAM BOOK.

This is the most complete dream book published. It contains an alphabetical list of dreams on every subject, including the lucky numbers, given names of both males and females and their numbers. Birthdays and their significance, Lucky Days, Rules to learn the number of saddles Gigs, and Horses in any given row of numbers, and what amount they will bring, Combination Tables, etc. It is the most reliable and authentic dream book ever published; the gathering of the material alone has occupied years of careful research. 208 pages.

Paper Covers........ .............. ............25 Cents
Cloth................. ................... ....50 Cents

Any book in this list sent postpaid to any address upon receipt of price.

Complete Catalogue sent free.

# FREDERICK J. DRAKE & CO., Publishers

## 211-213 EAST MADISON ST., CHICAGO

## COMIC RECITATIONS AND READINGS.

A new volume of Comic Readings and Recitations, compiled and edited by Charles Walter Brown, A. M., many of which have never been before published in book form. Its contents comprise some of the best efforts of such world-renowned humorists as Mark Twain, Josh Billings, Artemus Ward, Ezra Kendall, Bret Harte, Bill Nye, Ben King, Geo. Thatcher, Lew Dockstader, Wm. S. Gilbert, James Whitcomb Riley and others. This is an unequaled collection of the most amusing, eccentric, droll and humorous pieces, suitable for recitations in schools, drawing-room entertainments and amateur theatricals. 200 pages.

Paper Covers...................................... 25 Cents
Cloth, Gilt Titles................................. 50 Cents

## PATRIOTIC READINGS AND RECITATIONS

By Josephine Stafford. This is the choicest, newest and most complete collection of Patriotic recitations published, and includes all of the best known selections, together with the best utterances of all eminent statesmen. Selections for Decoration Day, Fourth of July, Washington's and Lincoln's birthdays, Arbor Day, Labor Day, and all other Patriotic occasions.

There are few things more popular during National Holidays than entertainments and exhibitions, and there is scarcely anything more difficult to procure than new and meritorious material appropriate for such occasions. This book will fill every want. 200 pages.

Paper Covers....................................... 25 Cents
Cloth, Gilt Titles.................................. 50 Cents

## LITTLE FOLKS' SPEAKER

By Chas. Walter Brown, A. M. Containing cute and catchy pieces for recitations by small children of ten years and much younger, including Speeches of Welcome and short Epilogues for opening and closing Children's Entertainments. The subjects are such as delight the infantile mind, and the language, while child-like is not childish. All of the selections are new and fresh, many being specially written for this volume. It would be difficult to find another collection so replete with short, bright, cheery printed pieces as contained in this book. 128 pages.

Paper Covers........................................ 25 Cents
Cloth, Gilt Titles.................................. 50 Cents

Any book in this list sent postpaid to any address upon receipt of price
Complete Catalogue sent free.

# FREDERICK J. DRAKE & CO., Publishers
## CHICAGO

# HERRMANN'S BOOK OF MAGIC. By Herrmann.

Including a full expose of the Black Art. This is a practical treatise on how to perform modern tricks. Great care has been exercised by the author to include in this book only such tricks as have never before appeared in print. This assures the performer a secret and almost endless fund for suitable material to be used on all occasions. With little practice almost anyone can perform the more simple tricks, and with practice, as he becomes more adept. he can perform the most difficult. No book published contains a greater variety of material for conjurers and slight-of-hand performers than this book. 180 pages, 41 illustrations.

Paper Cover...................................25 Cents
Cloth, Gold Titles............................50 Cents

# "CARD SHARPERS, THEIR TRICKS EXPOSED, OR THE ART OF ALWAYS WINNING." By Robert-Houdin.

This volume was expressly written to "enlighten the dupes and there will be no more cheating."

In unveiling the tricks of card sharpers, the author and editor have included everything practiced by gamblers of all countries, they having spent years in following every crooked or cheating move made by them, which is fully explained by diagrams.

The book when read will inspire no thought beyond that of guarding the reader against the card tricks of sharpers. 200 pages, 24 illustrations.

Paper Coper, printed in three colors...Price, $ .50
Cloth Cover, designs in gold and inks.   "    1.00

# THE EXPERT AT THE CARD TABLE.

By S. W. Erdnase. Without doubt the very best and most up-to-date treatise on the numerous sleights used by gamblers, concluding with a thoroughly interesting chapter on Card Sleights and Tricks with Cards.

Among the various new gambler's sleights will be found many which will prove of excellent service to the progressive conjuror. 205 pages, 101 illustrations.

12mo, Cloth................................Price $1.00

Any book in this list sent postpaid to any address, upon receipt of price. Complete Catalogue sent free.

## FREDERICK J. DRAKE & CO., Publishers
### 211-213 EAST MADISON ST., · · · · · CHICAGO

# BECAUSE I LOVE YOU. — THE BOOK OF LOVE, COURTSHIP AND MARRIAGE.

It fully explains How Maidens Become Happy Wives and Bachelors Become Happy Husbands in a brief space of time and by easy methods. Also Complete Directions for Declaring Intentions, Accepting Vows and Retaining Affections both Before and After Marriage, describing the invitations, the dresses, the ceremony and the proper behavior of both bride and bridegroom, whether in public or behind the nuptial curtain. It also tells plainly how to begin courting, the way to get over bashfulness, the way to "sit up," the way to find a soft spot in the sweetheart's breast. This is just the treatise to be in the hands of every young bachelor or maiden, every married man or women, every widow or widower, young and old—in fact it is a complete marriage guide. 200 pages.

Paper Cover..................................25 Cents
Cloth, Gold Titles ..........................50 Cents

# CARD TRICKS. HOW TO DO THEM.

And principles of Sleight of Hand. By A. Roterberg. Fully illustrated. This book gives, with careful and easy instructions, the newest card tricks and slight-of-hand yet offered to professionals and amateurs. Not only does this book contain all of the new tricks, but nearly every one known is fully explained and exposed by explicit directions and carefully prepared illustrations. No more agreeable form of public or private amusement can be devised than that of successful card tricks. 170 pages, 80 fine illustrations.

Paper Covers.............................25 Cents
Cloth, Gold Titles........................50 Cents

# TRICKS WITH COINS. By T. Nelson Downs.

A full and complete expose (illustrated) of the Author's World-Famous Coin Creation, "The Miser's Dream," including the correct method of executing the Continuous Back and Front-Hand Palm.

A series of absolutely new Passes with Coins, including eleven distinct and different methods of causing the disappearance of a single coin.

This book contains a complete explanation, with illustrations of every Coin Trick known. Written in a plain, easy, comprehensive style, which makes it the very best book on coin tricks published. To the professional and amateur this book will be an interesting addition to the already great number of works on what many consider to be the most fascinating art of the period. 170 pages, 95 illustrations. Paper Cover..25cts. Cloth, Gold Titles..50cts.

Any book in this list sent postpaid to any address upon receipt of price. Complete Catalogue sent free.

# FREDERICK J. DRAKE & CO., Publishers
## 211-213 EAST MADISON ST., CHICAGO

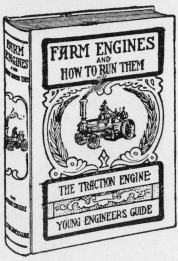

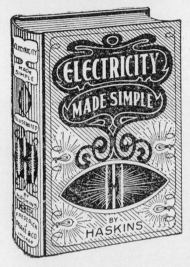

# BOOKKEEPING SELF-TAUGHT

## By *PHILLIP C. GOODWIN*

FEW, if any of of the technical works, which purport to be self-instructing have justified the claims made for them, and invariably the student either becomes discouraged and abandons his purpose and aim, or he is compelled to enlist the offices of a professional teacher, which in the great majority of instances is impracticable when considered in relation to the demands upon time and the condition of life to which the great busy public is subjected.

Mr. Goodwin's treatise on Bookkeeping is an entirely new departure from all former methods of self-instruction and one which can be studied systematically and alone by the student with quick and permanent results, or taken up in leisure moments with an absolute certainty of acquiring the science in a very short time and with little effort. The book is both a marvel of skill and simplicity. Every feature and every detail leading to the climax of scientific perfection are so thoroughly complete in this logical procedure and the analysis so thorough and deftly made that the self-teaching student is led by almost imperceptable, but sure and certain steps to the basic principles of the science, which the author in a most comprehensive and lucid style lays bare to intelligence of, even the most mediocre order.

The work is the most masterly exposition of the scientific principles of Bookkeeping and their practical application which has ever appeared in the English language, and it should be in the hands of every school boy or girl, every clerk, farmer, teacher and business or professional man; for a knowledge of Bookkeeping, even though it may not be followed as a profession, is a necessity felt by every person in business life and a recognized prime factor of business success.

In addition to a very simple yet elaborate explanation in detail of the systems of both single and double entry Bookkeeping, beginning with the initial transactions and leading the student along to the culminating exhibit of the balance sheet, the work contains a glossary of all the commercial terms employed in the business world, together with accounts in illustrative exercises for practice and one set of books completely written up.

12mo Cloth. Price $1.00.

Sent postpaid to any address upon receipt of price.

## Frederick J. Drake & Co., Publishers

### 211-213 EAST MADISON ST., CHICAGO

# Practical Lessons in Hypnotism *and* Magnetism

## By L. W. DE LAURENCE

Lecturer and Demonstrator at the De|Laurence Institute of Hypnotism and
Occult Philosophy, Chicago; author of "Medical Hypnosis,"
(Physicians' Edition); "The Bible Defended," etc.;
Student of the Orient in Practical Psychology,
Metaphysics, Alchemy, Cabala, Occult
and Natural Philosophy.

THIS is the author's **latest** and **best** work. It gives the only course which starts the student upon a plain, common sense basis of **Hypnotizing people.** Each of the many chapters contains practical lessons prepared especially for **self-instruction,** a feature never before offered the public. Many books published on Hypnotism pretend to teach the student without first mastering the real principles and entirely ignoring the constituent elements of Psychology. **Prof. De Laurence teaches a method which will enable any student to go right into a promiscuous audience without any subjects whom you have previously hypnotized, and give** SUCCESSFUL HYPNOTIC DEMONSTRATIONS. He has demonstrated the fact that anybody who can read can learn his methods as contained in this valuable book; the **instructions are plain** and the methods are the result of long experience, careful research and much study. THOUSANDS HAVE MASTERED HIS INSTRUCTIONS as taught in this book, and are now successfully applying it in their daily vocations, which is sufficient evidence to prove the worth of this volume. Fully illustrated.

Paper Covers . . . **$0.50**
Cloth, Gold Titles . . . **1.00**

Sold by Booksellers generally, or sent postpaid to any address upon receipt of price.

## FREDERICK J. DRAKE & CO., Publishers
### 211=213 East Madison St.,     CHICAGO

# Common-Sense Handrailings and How to Build Them

### By FRED T. HODGSON

*ILLUSTRATED*

THIS NEW VOLUME contains three distinct treatises on the subject, each of which is complete in itself. The system of forming the lines for obtaining the various curves, wreaths, ramps and face moulds for handrails are the simplest in use and those employed by the most successful handrailers. Mr. Hodgson has placed this unusually intricate subject before his readers in a very plain and easily understood manner, and any workman having a fair knowledge of "lines" and who can construct an ordinary straight stairway can readily grasp the whole system of "handrailing" after a small study of this work.

The building of stairs and properly making and placing over them a graceful handrail and suitable balusters and newel posts is one of the greatest achievements of the joiner's art and skill, yet it is an art that is the least understood of any of the constructive processes the carpenter or joiner is called upon to accomplish. In but very few of the plans made by an architect are the stairs properly laid down or divided off; indeed, most of the stairs as laid out and planned by the architect, are impossible ones owing to the fact that the circumstances that govern the formation of the rail, are either not understood, or not noticed by the designer, and the expert handrailer often finds it difficult to conform the stairs and rail to the plan. Generally, however, he gets so close to it that the character of the design is seldom changed.

The stairs are the great feature of a building as they are the first object that meets the visitor and claims his attention, and it is essential, therefore, that the stair and its adjuncts should have a neat and graceful appearance, and this can only be accomplished by having the rail properly made and set up.

This little book gives such instructions in the art of handrailing as will enable the young workman to build a rail so that it will assume a handsome appearance when set in place. There are eleven distinct styles of stairs shown, but the same principle that governs the making of the simplest rail, governs the construction of the most difficult, so, once having mastered the simple problems in this system, progress in the art will become easy, and a little study and practice will enable the workman to construct a rail for the most tortuous stairway.

The book is copiously illustrated with nearly one hundred working diagrams together with full descriptive text.

### 12mo CLOTH, PRICE, $1.00

**FREDERICK J. DRAKE & CO., Publishers**
**CHICAGO**